WORLD BANK WORKING PAPER NO. 156

Developing the Workforce, Shaping the Future

Transformation of Madagascar's Post-basic Education

Sajitha Bashir

Africa Region Human Development Department

THE WORLD BANK
Washington, D.C.

Copyright © 2009
The International Bank for Reconstruction and Development / The World Bank
1818 H Street, N.W.
Washington, D.C. 20433, U.S.A.
All rights reserved
Manufactured in the United States of America
First Printing: January 2009

 printed on recycled paper

1 2 3 4 5   12 11 10 09

World Bank Working Papers are published to communicate the results of the Bank's work to the development community with the least possible delay. The manuscript of this paper therefore has not been prepared in accordance with the procedures appropriate to formally-edited texts. Some sources cited in this paper may be informal documents that are not readily available.

The findings, interpretations, and conclusions expressed herein are those of the author(s) and do not necessarily reflect the views of the International Bank for Reconstruction and Development/The World Bank and its affiliated organizations, or those of the Executive Directors of The World Bank or the governments they represent.

The World Bank does not guarantee the accuracy of the data included in this work. The boundaries, colors, denominations, and other information shown on any map in this work do not imply any judgment on the part of The World Bank of the legal status of any territory or the endorsement or acceptance of such boundaries.

The material in this publication is copyrighted. Copying and/or transmitting portions or all of this work without permission may be a violation of applicable law. The International Bank for Reconstruction and Development/The World Bank encourages dissemination of its work and will normally grant permission promptly to reproduce portions of the work.

For permission to photocopy or reprint any part of this work, please send a request with complete information to the Copyright Clearance Center, Inc., 222 Rosewood Drive, Danvers, MA 01923, USA, Tel: 978-750-8400, Fax: 978-750-4470, www.copyright.com.

All other queries on rights and licenses, including subsidiary rights, should be addressed to the Office of the Publisher, The World Bank, 1818 H Street NW, Washington, DC 20433, USA, Fax: 202-522-2422, email: pubrights@worldbank.org.

ISBN-13: 978-0-8213-7816-8
eISBN: 978-0-8213-7817-5
ISSN: 1726-5878   DOI: 10.1596/978-0-8213-7816-8

Library of Congress Cataloging-in-Publication Data has been requested.

Contents

Foreword vii
Acknowledgments ix
Acronyms and Abbreviations xi
Executive Summary xiii

1. Introduction 1

2. Trends in Enrollment and Completion 7

3. Education–Labor Market Linkages 17

4. Skills for the Labor Market: Improving Relevance and Quality
   in Post-basic Education and Training 31

5. Access and Equity in Post-basic Education 51

6. Partnerships for Growth: Innovation and On-the-Job Training 67

7. Adapting to Change: Issues and Reforms in Public Expenditure
   and Finance Management 79

8. Steering Change: Reforms in Management and Governance 93

9. A Strategic Framework for Post-basic Education in Madagascar 101

Appendix: The Reform of Basic Education in Madagascar:
Lessons and Implications for Post-basic Education 109

Statistical Annex 115
Table 1. Public and Private Enrollment by Educational Sub-Sector, 1997–2006 116
Table 2. Schools and Teachers by Cycle 117
Table 3. Average Years of Education of the Employed Labor Force by Age Group 118
Table 4. Earnings Regression: Salary/Wage Earners, All Sectors, 2001 and 2005 119
Table 5. Earnings Regression: Salary/Wage Earners, Industrial Sector, 2005 121
Table 6. Estimated Stochastic Production Frontier Models, 2004 123
Table 7. Public Expenditures on Education by Sub-Sector (Ariary) 124
Table 8. Public Expenditures on Education by Sub-Sector (US$) 125

References 127

LIST OF TABLES, FIGURES, AND BOXES

TABLES

1. Madagascar: Net Enrollment Rates per Income Level in 2001 and 2005 (%) 15
2. Growth Sector Skill Needs and Labor Supply 33
3. Types of Public Financing for Private Schools 63
4. Madagascar's Global Competitiveness Index Rankings, 2007–08 68
5. Madagascar's GCI Rankings for Higher Education and Training, 2007 69
6. Madagascar's GCI Rankings for Innovation, 2007 69
7. Innovation Indicators for Madagascar's Formal Sector Manufacturing Firms, 2005 71
8. Determinants of the Decision to Train Employees in the Formal Manufacturing Sector, 2004 74
9. Determinants of Training and Impact on Earnings, Formal Industry Sector 2005 75
10. Allocation of Public Education Expenditure by Sub-sector, 2002–07 81
11. Allocation of Public Capital Expenditures in Education by Sub-sector, 2002–07 ... 82
12. Per Student Public Recurrent Expenditure, by Level of Education, Constant 2006 Prices 83
13. Two Scenarios for Government Regulation 99
14. Framework for Strategic Development of Post-basic Education 106

FIGURES

1. Education and the Commitments of the MAP 2
2. Students in Higher Education, 1969–2006 4
3. Planned Reform to Basic Education Curriculum 5
4a. Primary Enrollment, 1997–2007 8
4b. Junior Secondary Enrollment, 1997–2007 8
4c. SSE, TVET, and HE Enrollment, 1997–2007 8
5. International Comparison of Gross Enrollment Rates, Secondary and Higher Education, 2005 9
6. Share of Private Sector in Enrollment by Sub-sector, 1997–2007 9
7. Entry into Higher Education by Baccalauréat Series, 2005–06 10
8. First-year University Dropout Rates by University, 2004–05 11
9. Student Survival, JSE to Higher Education 13
10. Distribution of the Population by Highest Educational Attainment and Income, 2004 14
11. Madagascar: Labor Status of the Population, 2005 18
12. Cross-country Comparison of Adult Educational Attainment, 2001–05 19
13. Average Years of Education by Age Group, Employed Labor Force, 2001 and 2005 20

14. Educational Attainment of Employed Labor Force Participants Under Age 30, 2001 and 2005 21
15. Share of Population That Has Attained at Least Grade 5 by Age Group, 2005 21
16a. Share of Population That Has Attained at Least Grade 9 by Age Group, 2005 22
16b. Share of Population That Has Attained at Least Grade 12 by Age Group, 2005 22
17. Distribution of Employed Labor Force by Highest Qualification Obtained and Annual Education/Training Awards, 2005 23
18. Educational Attainment of Employed Labor Forces by Region, 2005 24
19. Education Levels in MAP Target Regions, 2005 25
20. Return to Education by Educational Level, Wage and Salary Earners, 2005 27
21. Typology of Technological Occupations in the Knowledge Economy 34
22. Madagascar's Senior Secondary Education (SSE) Cycle 36
23. Structure of Madagascar TVET system, 2007 (Pre-reform) 40
24. Graduates of Applied Science, Engineering, and Technology Programs, 2005–06 44
25. NIOS Process for Learning System Development 56
26. Private Education in Madagascar 59
27. Share of Private Sector in Secondary Education Institutions, by Region 60
28. Distribution of Private School Enrollment by Type of Institution, 2005–06 61
29. Madagascar Knowledge Indicators: Innovation Systems 70
30. Select Knowledge Indicators: Madagascar and Middle-income SADC Countries ... 71
31. Total Public Education Expenditure as Percent of GDP, 1996–2006 80
32. Investment Spending in SSE, TVET, and Higher Education, by Source of Financing, 2006 82
33. Composition of Recurrent Public Expenditure by Education Sub-sector, 2007 84
34. Composition of Transfers for Higher Education, by Category of Expenditure, 2006 84
35. Composition of Recurrent Expenditure in Higher Education, 2006 85
36. Supplementary Hours as Percent of Total University Teaching Hours, 2006 86
37. New Structure of Basic Education 110
38. Proposed Curriculum, Grades 1–10 111

Boxes

1. Observations on the Availability of Middle Managers and Skilled Technicians 28
2. Alternative Models for Secondary Education 39
3. Strategies for Shifting to LMD in Selected European Countries 46
4. Main Features of the National Institute of Open School, India 57
5. Ten Characteristics of Successful Open Universities 58
6. Model for a Post-basic Education Reform Commission 94

Foreword

Sub-Saharan African countries are increasingly recognizing the contribution of post-basic education to economic growth and social development. However, policy makers in many poor countries struggle to balance expansion and upgrading of post-basic education reform against competing development priorities. They must consider how—and sometimes whether—to fund post-basic education in the face of demographic growth, limited public resources, and political and social imperatives.

In its new poverty reduction and growth strategy, the Madagascar Action Plan (MAP), the Government of Madagascar made the transformation of its education system one of the key pillars of its development agenda. An important decision was the reform of basic education, covering primary and junior secondary education, including extension of the basic education cycle to 10 years. The Government's new Education for All (EFA) Plan provides the policy framework and operational strategies for basic education, covering changes to curricula and learning materials, teaching methods and student assessment. The EFA Plan was endorsed by donors and the reform of basic education launched in 2008.

However, basic education reform alone cannot fuel Madagascar's growth. Madagascar's work force needs a higher average skill level and different types of skills to compete with other countries in the global market. Today, Madagascar's post-basic education system is not up to the challenge; plagued by decades of neglect and low investment, it performs poorly, in terms of the number and quality of its graduates.

The Government of Madagascar recognizes that significant reform of post-basic education is required to face up to the challenges, but also that trade-offs and prioritization will be necessary. This study was undertaken to support the government's efforts to develop a strategy for creating a post-basic education and training system which is more flexible and responsive to labor market needs, and which can support and shape the growth agenda. The study reviews the performance of Madagascar's post-basic education and training system and identifies reform priorities, medium term policy goals and strategies for increasing access, quality and relevance.

The study covers senior secondary, technical/vocational, and higher education. It is structured around three broad topics: (i) improving the quality and relevance of the post-basic education and training system and its contribution to skill development and knowledge transfer in a changing economic environment; (ii) identifying cost-effective measures for increasing access to post-basic education, including greater equity; and (iii) proposing key reforms in financing, management and governance of education and training at the level of institutions and the system as a whole.

The study has already provided useful inputs for developing the national post-basic education strategy. It is also a good example of collaboration between the World Bank and the Government, who worked together to identify core problems in post-basic education and to develop solutions to address those problems. I hope that the broad distribution of this study will enrich the debate across all stakeholders who support a modern education system in Madagascar, and strong post-basic education systems across Sub-Saharan Africa as a whole.

Yaw Ansu
Director, Human Development, Africa Region, The World Bank

Acknowledgments

This study was prepared by Sajitha Bashir (Senior Education Economist, AFTH3), with key contributions from Jamil Salmi (Lead Education Specialist, HDNED) on higher education and Patrick Ramanantoanina (Senior Education Specialist, AFTH3) on secondary education. Background papers for the study were commissioned by the World Bank and the Ministry of Education and Scientific Research, Government of Madagascar (*Ministère de l'Education Nationale*—MEN). These include papers by Gerard Lassibille (consultant on education and labor market analysis, World Bank), David Stifel (consultant for household survey analysis, World Bank), Sam Mikhail (consultant on higher education, World Bank), Richard Johanson (consultant on technical and vocational education/training, World Bank), S.N. Prasad (consultant for study of curriculum development and textbooks in Indian states, World Bank), Rohen d'Aiglepierre (consultant on private sector education, jointly financed by World Bank and Agence Française de Développement), John Middleton (consultant on secondary education, MEN) and Hafedh Zaafrane (consultant on higher education costs and financing, MEN). The report also draws on analyses done by the MEN team on the Country Status Report on Education (in progress), supported by the Bank team led by Mamy Rakotomalala (Senior Education Specialist, AFTH3). Hope Neighbor (consultant, World Bank) prepared the first draft of the Executive Summary and designed final charts, diagrams and tables. Chie Ingvoldstad (consultant, World Bank) provided valuable research assistance and proofing of the report. The final formatting was done by Norosoa Andrianaivo (Program Assistant, AFTH3).

The findings of various background papers were discussed with the MEN team at various stages. The study benefited from these discussions, specifically with Haja Nirina Razafinjatovo (Minister of Finances and Budget and former Minister of Education and Scientific Research), Andriamparany Benjamin Radavidson (former Minister of Education and Scientific Research), Ying Vah Zafilahy (Vice-Minister of Education, in charge of higher education and vocational training), Harry Serge Raheriniaina (former General Secretary, Ministry of Education), Ridjanirainy Randrianarisoa (former General Secretary, Ministry of Education), Minoson Rakotomalala (Director of Cabinet, Ministry of Education), Romain Kleber Andrianjafy (General Secretary, Ministry of Education), Tahinarinoro Razafindramary (Director-General of basic education, Ministry of Education), Christian Guy Ralijaona (Director-General of higher education and research, Ministry of Education), Harisoa Andriamihamina Rasolonjatovo (Coordinator of the Technical Working Group, Ministry of Education), Josoa Ramamonjisoa (Director of Higher Institute of Technology) and Josiane Rabetokotany (Technical Coordinator of Education for All).

On the Bank side, the study benefited from comments and guidance from Laura Frigenti (Country Director, Central America), Robert Blake (Country Manager, Madagascar), Ritva Reinikaa (Sector Director, MNSED), Jee-Peng Tan (Education Adviser, AFTHD) and Ganesh Rasagam (Senior Private Sector Development Specialist, AFTFP). The two peer reviewers, Shahid Yusuf (Economic Adviser, DECRG) and Juan Manuel Moreno (Senior Education Specialist, ECSHD), provided comments on the Concept Note and the final draft of the report.

Financial support from the Norwegian Post Primary Education Fund for various background studies is gratefully acknowledged.

Acronyms and Abbreviations

AESPHM	*L'Association des Établissements Supérieurs Privés Homologués* (The Association of the Approved Private Higher Establishments)
ASET	Applied Science Engineering and Technology
CFP	*Centres de Formation Professionnelle* (Vocational Training Centers)
CISCO	*Circonscription Scolaire* (School District)
CNEP	*Commission Nationale de l'Enseignement Privé* (National Commission of Private Teaching)
CNTEMAD	*Centre National de Télé-enseignement de Madagascar* (Madagascar Distance Learning Center)
COE	*Collège d'excellence* (Junior Secondary School)
CP	*Centre Professionnelle* (Vocational Center)
CROU	*Centres Régionaux des Œuvres Universitaires* (Regional Centers of University Works)
CNFTP	*Conseil National de la Formation Technique Professionnelle* (National Council of Technical and Vocational Training)
DN	*Direction Nationale* (National Direction)
DREN	*Direction Régionale de l'Education Nationale* (Regional direction of National Education)
EFA	Education for All
ENS	*Ecoles Normales Supérieures* (Higher General Education)
FDI	Foreign Direct Investment
FRAM	*Fikambanan'ny Ray Aman-drenin'ny Mpianatra* (Parents Students Association)
GCI	Global Competitiveness Index
GDP	Gross Domestic Product
GEETP	*Groupement des Etablissements d'Enseignement Technique et Professionnel* (Technical and Professional Educational Establishments Group)
GER	Gross Enrollment Ratio
HE	Higher Education
HEI	Higher Education Institution
ICA	Investment Climate Assessment
ICT	Information and Communication Technology
IDA	International Development Association
INFOR	*Institut National de Formation* (National Institute of Training)
INSTAT	*Institut National de Statistiques* (National Institute of Statistics)
INTH	*Institut National de Tourisme et d'Hôtellerie* (National Institute of Tourism and Hotel Trade)
ISCAM	*L'Institut Supérieure de la Communication, des Affaires et du Management* (The Higher Institute of Communication, Businesses and Management)
IST	*Institut Supérieure de Technologie* (Higher Institute of Technology)

JSE	Junior Secondary Education
KAM	Knowledge Assessment Methodology
LMD	*Licence-Maitrîse-Doctorat* (Bachelor's/Master's/Doctorate)
LTP	*Lycée Technique Professionnelle* (Technical/Vocational High School)
MAP	Madagascar Action Plan
MEN	*Ministère de l'Education Nationale* (Ministry of National Education)
NIOS	National Institute of Open Schooling
NTA	National Training Authority
ODL	Open and Distance Learning
ONEP	*Office Nationale de l'Enseignement Privé* (National Office of Private Education)
R&D	Research and Development
SADC	Southern Africa Development Community
SSA	Sub-Saharan Africa
SSE	Senior Secondary Education
TVET	Technical and Vocational Education and Training
UNESCO	United Nations Educational Scientific and Cultural Organization
USPTO	United States Patents and Trademarks Office
WEF	World Economic Forum

Education and Training Qualifications

BAC	*Baccalauréat* (SSE final examination)
BACPRO	*Baccalauréat Professionnel* (Professional SSE final examination)
BEP	*Brevet d'Etude Professionnelle* (Professional Study Diploma)
BEPC	*Brevet d'Etudes du Premier Cycle* (JSE final examination)
BT	*Baccalauréat Technologique* (Technological SSE final examination)
BTS	*Brevet de Technicien Supérieur* (High-level Technician Diploma)
CAP	*Certificat d'Aptitude Professionnelle* (Vocational Aptitude Certificate)
CEPE	*Certificat d'Etudes Primaires et Elémentaires* (Primary School Leaving Certificate)
CFA	*Certificat de Fin d'Apprentissage* (End of Training Certificate)
DEA	*Diplôme d'Études Approfondis* (Doctoral Qualifying Degree)
DESS	*Diplôme d'Etudes Supérieures Spécialisées* (Diploma of Higher Education Specialist)
DEUG	*Diplôme d'Études Universitaire Générale* (BAC+2) (Diploma of General Higher Education)
DIIST	*Diplôme d'Ingénieur de l'IST* (Engineer Diploma of IST)
DTS	*Diplôme de Technicien Supérieur* (High-level Technician Diploma)
DTSS	*Diplôme de Technicien Supérieur Spécialisé* (High-level Specialized Technician Diploma)
DUT	*Diplôme d'Etudes Technologiques* (Diploma in Technology)
LP	*Licence Professionnelle* (Professional Bachelor's Degree)

Executive Summary

Demand for Reform of Post-Basic Education

The transformation of education is one of the eight pillars of the 2007–11 Madagascar Action Plan (MAP), the country's new development strategy. Consistent with this focus, the Government announced a major re-structuring of school education in 2005 and has completed a plan for basic education reform, covering seven years of primary and three years of junior secondary education. The Government is now starting to prepare a strategy for post-basic education. The main purpose of this report is to provide analytical inputs for the development of post-basic education reforms. Specifically, the report identifies and prioritizes: (i) the need for change in the structure, content and delivery of Madagascar's post-basic education and training system, and (ii) the key reforms in financing, governance and sub-sector management required to support changes to the structure, content and delivery of the post-basic system.

Madagascar's challenges are enormous. Education indicators at the post-basic level rank it among the lowest performing countries in the world. The gross enrollment ratio in senior secondary education (SSE) is just 10 percent, and in tertiary education less than 3 percent. Public resources are limited, especially at the post-primary level. The tax:GDP ratio is about 11 percent, one of the lowest in sub-Saharan Africa. The government budget is highly dependent on donor funding. Within the education sector, both domestic allocations and donor funding are heavily biased towards primary education in order to ensure universal primary completion, which is currently less than 60 percent.

The MAP outlines an ambitious development strategy, focusing on promoting investment in high growth sectors and regional development. If successful, it will change the demand for skills in fundamental ways. Since 2005, foreign direct investment has increased rapidly. Unless the post-basic education system adapts to the changing demand for skills and other services, it may hinder Madagascar's ability to meet the objectives of the MAP.

Core Challenges for Reform

At present, Madagascar's post-basic education and training system is not able to meet the demands of a changing economy for five core reasons. These reasons include: (i) poor quality and relevance; (ii) low attainment and inequity in access; (iii) internal inefficiency of the education system; (iv) financial inefficiency (under-funded, high cost); and (v) a weak enabling framework (financial management, governance).

Poor Quality and Relevance

Madagascar's post-basic education and training system does not provide graduates with skills that are relevant in today's—or tomorrow's—labor markets. Madagascar's secondary education curriculum was last reformed in the 1970s. Its curriculum structure is highly academic and overloaded: the series in the general and technological/technical *baccalauréats* do not correspond to the disciplines and skills that are now important in the economy. Both technical/vocational education and training and higher education have inflexible long duration courses. The former provides a limited range of technical skills for narrowly defined occupations. In higher education, Madagascar has not introduced the *bachelor's-master's-Ph.D* system to which most European countries have transitioned over the last 10 years, although the plans for implementing this system have been developed. Both the curriculum and curriculum structure contribute to high rates of exam failure, repetition and dropout. Equally importantly, the curriculum fails to build flexible "employability" skills that graduates can apply to problem solving in many areas. Linkages between education and training institutions and industry/employers in the private sector are limited, both in research and in enterprise-based training. As a result, Madagascar ranks low in international competitiveness (the Global Competitiveness Index ranks Madagascar 118 out of 131 countries ranked overall, and 121 on higher education and training).

Internal Inefficiency

The education system is inefficient at all levels, starting with primary education. High rates of dropout, repetition and exam failure mean that very few students complete each cycle. As a result, although grade 6 enrollment is currently 189,000, Madagascar produces just 4,200 higher education graduates per year. The pass rate for the *baccalauréat* examination is just over 40 percent. The pass rate for first year university exams is just 50 percent, contributing to high drop-out. Repetition rates average 14 percent in post-basic education. These rates imply a very high wastage of resources that Madagascar can ill afford, and result in a growing number of out-of-school youth with limited educational attainment.

Low Attainment and Inequity in Access

Madagascar's human capital stock is very low, reflecting the cumulative effect of years of low enrollment and high rates of drop-out, repetition, and exam failure. One measure of human capital is the educational attainment of the labor force. In 2005, the average years of education was 4 years. Only 1.7 percent of the working age population had post-secondary education, and only 9 percent had secondary education. Moreover, investment in human capital has not followed a steady upward trend. The proportion of the population that had attained grade 12 peaked about 20 years ago, at 6 percent, but had dropped to 3 percent by 2005. Labor market indicators suggest that there is no immediate national skill shortage, due to the small size of the formal sector. Nonetheless, upgrading the skill composition of Madagascar's labor force is a strategic imperative, necessary for supporting the government's growth strategy of poverty reduction and regional development.

Inequity in access is related to both income levels and regional disparities. The secondary net enrollment rate for children from the poorest 60 percent of households is less than 8 percent. Only 1 percent of children from the poorest 20 percent of households is enrolled in tertiary education. Only two regions have close to 10 percent of workers with at least senior secondary education. Only one of the eight regions targeted by the MAP (Analamanga) has a level of tertiary education of more than 5 percent. Because Madagascar has poor quality infrastructure, internal migration cannot compensate for the lack of local skilled labor supply.

Financial Inefficiency

Post-basic education is under-funded and high cost. The share of public education expenditure allocated to post-primary sub-sectors is low in absolute terms (SSE: 5.5 percent; TVET: 2.3 percent; tertiary: 15.6 percent), and when compared francophone and anglophone SSA countries. Furthermore, the curriculum structure and specialization drive high costs by increasing teacher and classroom requirements. Finally, the remaining resources are used inefficiently. Spending on post-basic is largely committed to teacher salaries, in large part due to low "regular" teaching loads. Indicatively, 98.7 percent of SSE and 78 percent of TVET recurrent expenditure is allocated to personnel costs and other staff payments. In higher education, faculty members are paid supplementary hours for teaching more than five hours a week, which creates a strong incentive for faculty to teach additional hours. Supplementary teaching hours now exceeds regular teaching hours by a factor of 4:1 and result in high levels of spending on supplementary payments to teachers. This, in turn, limits funding available for teacher training, curriculum, or materials development—investments that would help to improve educational quality and outcomes.

Weak Enabling Framework

A weak enabling framework, including poor governance and budget management, presents the final challenge to improvement of Madagascar's post-basic education and training system.

In terms of governance, the biggest issue has been the lack of effective leadership and vision in steering the post-basic education sector. *High level political leadership and broad-based consensus are critical to successful education reform. Instead of creating the stability required to undertake change, the Ministry of Education has frequently changed its organizational structure.* The Ministry has limited professional capacity to develop policy, operational strategies and implementation plans. Finally, there is no "feedback loop" between MEN and the economic sector, meaning that post-basic education is not responsive to current or future economic needs.

Despite the recent move to "program" budgets, there is a lack of capacity to prepare budgets according to strategic priorities. Separate preparation and reporting is still required for the three main parts of the budget (personnel, non-personnel, and public investment program expenditure). Delays in budget execution are frequent and budget reporting is extremely weak, with virtually no oversight of expenditures in educational institutions.

Priorities for Action

Madagascar's "core challenges" and the window of opportunity provided by the implementation of basic education reform imply that reform must improve the quality and relevance of post-basic education, while putting cost-effective mechanisms for expanding access in place. Post-basic reform should not focus exclusively on a massive expansion of the existing post-basic system. Instead, successful reform will: (i) focus first on improving educational content (structure, curriculum, teaching, and process) and linkages with the economy; (ii) increase coverage, cost-effectively; and (iii) strengthen the enabling framework for reform (governance, finance, and sub-sector management).

Improve Educational Content and Linkages with the Economy

Reforms aimed at improving educational content must accomplish three objectives: (i) meet the skilled labor requirements of the economy's key growth sectors, in the short to medium term; (ii) gradually build professional capabilities in the key growth sectors, also in the short to medium term; and (iii) help youth to develop the knowledge, skills and attitudes—"employability skills"—that will allow them to participate in and adapt to the changing labor market over time.

Senior secondary education. Senior secondary reform should focus on two pillars. The first pillar would focus on incremental, school-based reforms. The main change would be to simplify the curriculum, and to make it more relevant to labor market needs. This could include reducing subject overload; re-organizing the *baccalauréats* into more relevant tracks; and upgrading curricular content to include employability skills and knowledge in core subjects. These changes could be accompanied by changes to teacher training (teaching practices) and learning materials. Reforms aimed at improving teacher quality could include school-based in-service teacher development; design of a teacher certification that could be open to all bachelor's or master's degree holders, not only those who have studied pedagogy at the university level; and expansion of tertiary institutions' capacity to train teacher educators.

A second pillar would introduce new types of secondary and vocational schools, more closely aligned with labor market needs in MAP priority sectors. Measures to improve economic and regional equality would be built into each pillar. These measures would include a new school development fund, targeting disadvantaged regions, and equity-focused criteria for scholarship programs and school construction or renovation.

TVET. Six reforms are important to enabling TVET to train students on relevant, in-demand labor market skills. These reforms include: (i) beginning vocational training after 10 years of basic education; (ii) expanding technical training at the senior secondary level (and scaling back training at the junior secondary level); (iii) involving regions and communes in training decisions, to balance the distribution of training across regions and to ensure that training responds to local labor market needs; (iv) introducing new courses for priority sectors; (v) enhancing subject-area learning; and (vi) improving the quality of instruction through pre- and in-service teacher training.

Tertiary education. Reforms to improve the quality of higher education could include: (i) selection of undergraduate courses and disciplines that are important to Madagascar's economic development; (ii) expansion of short courses for training higher level technicians; (iii) accelerated introduction of the shift towards a progressive *bachelor's-master's-PhD* system; and (iv) partnership with foreign universities to build local institutional capacity and to leverage international experience.

Reforms in higher education can also encourage research. On-going research is critical to innovation and growth, but has been neglected in recent years. Research can be spurred by: (i) building a cadre of young researchers in priority fields; (ii) funding research competitively and selectively, to solve problems that are important to national and regional economic development; and (iii) encouraging contract research, particularly for foreign firms operating in Madagascar.

Changes to faculty hiring and development are critical to improving both quality and research capabilities at the university level. Madagascar must develop clear standards for recruiting the required numbers of high quality faculty, estimated in the hundreds. Selection criteria should include expertise in a key growth discipline, such as math, science or language; PhD candidacy or completion; significant time remaining in the career; and successful completion of a trial teaching or research period. Faculty development might include workshops designed to upgrade faculty skills in the short term, and research support in the long term.

Increasing Coverage, Cost-effectively

There are four viable channels for expanding enrollment in post-basic education. These include: (i) more effective cost management; (ii) equitable, efficient scholarship programs; (iii) open and distance learning programs; and (iv) greater private sector provision of education.

Cost management. A short list of initiatives will help Madagascar to use its post-basic education budget more efficiently. In SSE, teacher utilization could be improved by reforming the curriculum; planning new school locations carefully; and increasing the size of urban schools. A school construction strategy, building on the experience of national school construction strategy for basic education, could create clear norms for the location and technical quality of new schools. In TVET, resources could be used more efficiently by shortening the length of training. In tertiary education, MEN might evaluate the feasibility of expanding enrollment to 5,000 students or more per university. MEN might also consolidate post-graduate programs to 1–2 universities, to achieve economies of scale.

Equitable, efficient scholarship programs. Madagascar's existing university-level scholarships were originally designed to help the neediest students. By 2006, 83 percent of tertiary students were granted scholarships. Because almost all tertiary students are from the top income quintile, tertiary scholarships effectively provide an income subsidy to this quintile. There are no scholarships at the senior secondary level. To enhance poor students' access to higher education, the Government might: (i) provide scholarship amounts that meet the actual living costs of those who are not able to pay; (ii) define stricter, more needs-based eligibility criteria; (iii) consider needs-based scholarships to private universities; (iv) link scholarship renewal to academic performance; and (v) undertake a feasibility study on the establishment of a student loan system. Scholarships should also be introduced at the secondary level, to improve equity by increasing secondary enrollment among rural students and those from educationally under-served districts.

Open and distance learning programs (ODL). ODL programs expand access at the secondary and tertiary levels by introducing flexibility for those who have been unable to continue their formal education. Madagascar is actively considering creation of ODL programs. The first step in introducing ODL programs should be a feasibility study, to decide on the appropriate ODL model for Madagascar in terms of programs, learners, delivery mechanisms, tech platforms, and business model. Features of successful ODL programs include relevance, self-financing over a few years' time, and clear, professional management structures.

Expanded private sector provision of education. Private education provides a fourth means of cost-effectively expanding access to post-basic education. Private institutions enroll a significant proportion of students in post-basic education. In 2006/07, the private sector share was 54 percent of SSE, 39 percent of JSE, and 64 percent of technical/vocational. Further expansion could be encouraged in urban areas, which would allow the Government to concentrate public resources on improving access to under-served areas and groups. The regulatory framework for private secondary schools is relatively clear, but the framework for private technical/vocational and higher education institutions is not well-defined. Finally, existing subsidies to private institutions benefit mainly the primary level, and are not well targeted and do not have clear objectives. To support increased private sector participation in post-basic education, the Government might: (i) clarify and communicate procedures for establishing and recognizing schools; (ii) rationalize subsidy programs for secondary schools; and (iii) build central and local capacity to develop private education. In technical/vocational and higher education, the priority should be on finalizing and approving the procedures for private schools' recognition and accreditation.

Strengthen the Enabling Framework for Reform

Reforms in system governance, financial management and post-basic sub-sectors will enable the Government to build the capacity to carry out post-basic reform more effectively.

Governance. Governance reforms might focus on the following areas: (i) building mechanisms for political leadership of the reform; (ii) re-defining the role of the Ministry of Education; and (iii) creating a National Qualifications Framework.

Many countries have found it useful to create *mechanisms for strong political leadership of the reform.* Madagascar could consider establishing a commission for post-basic education, to build high-level political support and broad-based consensus for change.

To *re-define the role of Ministry of Education,* the Government might carry out an institutional assessment of key structures in the Ministry. It might also identify capacity building measures for key functions such as planning, budgeting, human resource management, and project management.

Creation of a *National Qualifications Framework* would ensure that post-basic education and training reflects current and future labor market needs, and that post-basic credentials are recognized and respected in the labor market. A National Qualifications Framework could provide a hierarchy of educational qualifications that clearly describes the knowledge and skills gained from each post-basic degree, and the equivalency between degrees. It could serve as a consistent framework that employers could use to identify prospective employees' knowledge and skills. It would also allow educational institutions to target program admissions, curriculum and exams to different skill standards. Common elements of this framework might include: industry identification of relevant occupations, and skills and knowledge required to be trained for those occupations; curriculum, teacher training and learning materials required to meet the skills standards; accreditation of each program, to ensure that skill standards are met; and definition of a hierarchy of qualifications, based on stakeholder input and designed to determine equivalence and progression.

Financial management. There are three areas where the Ministry of Education might enhance financial management. First, it might explore means of increasing cost-sharing, particularly in financing of textbooks and learning materials (to be offset by measures for poor children). Second, in technical/vocational and higher education, resource mobilization from employers and students should be encouraged. The Ministry of Education should provide public institutions, particularly universities, with clear rules that govern how private resources are mobilized, used and accounted for. Third, MEN might explore the development of mechanisms that link increases in public funding of higher education to performance improvements. These might include output-based funding formulas, linking funding to indicators of institutional performance; performance contracts; or competitive funds, awarded to peer-reviewed proposals for improving institutional performance, innovation and management.

Sub-sector reforms include reforms specific to SSE, TVET and higher education. At the *SSE level,* schools lack the autonomy to make decisions or allocate budget against school needs or priorities. These gaps cannot be effectively filled by MEN centrally. School development funds and/or scholarship programs would allow schools to address their own needs directly. In *TVET,* there is limited opportunity for employers to provide input on post-basic education. The Government might create mechanisms to facilitate this communication, including national training authorities, "sector councils" in key sectors, or training needs assessments carried out in conjunction with investment promotion. There are four reform priorities for *higher education.* First, MEN might move from direct management functions to a more strategic role (for example, vision-setting, medium-term planning). Second, MEN could grant increased managerial authority to the public tertiary institutions under its authority, accompanied by agreed performance objectives. Third, the composition and powers of university boards could be re-structured, so that boards combine supervisory and executive responsibilities. Fourth, the Government might move ahead with its accreditation system for public and private institutions.

Cost of reform. Post-basic education reform must also be realistic and financially sustainable. The Ministry needs to develop alternate scenarios for reform, and cost each alternative. This will make trade-offs between the scope and cost of the reform explicit, allowing the Ministry to identify the best possible reform alternative.

A Timeframe for the Reform Program

The following timeframe is suggested for designing and implementing reforms:

- *Short term (1–2 years):* (i) determine strategic policy choices; (ii) cost the alternative reform scenarios, to assess the financial sustainability of each scenario; (iii) choose a reform scenario, to guide budget allocation and additional donor funding; (iv) design new governance structures and financing instruments, to orient the system towards labor market needs and to improve equity; (v) launch investment on a modest scale for quality improvement in selected institutions and programs, devolving greater autonomy to institutions, and (vi) diversify types of programs/institutions
- *Medium term (3–5 years):* (i) establish a National Qualifications Framework; (ii) revise the regulatory framework for the private sector, accreditation and other system level structures; (iii) increase the use of performance-based financing instruments to reinforce reforms at the institution level; and (iv) expand the investment program to upgrade quality, create some model new institutions, and enhance access
- *Long term (beyond 5 years):* (i) update the National Qualifications Framework, based on feedback from employers, educational institutions and end beneficiaries; (ii) create governance systems for permanent interaction between MEN and employers, and sustainable financing mechanisms; (iii) ensure all education and training institutions are accredited and become autonomous; and (iv) roll out quality improvement reforms throughout the system and expand access rapidly.

CHAPTER 1

Introduction

Objectives and Background

The main aim of the study is to provide analytical inputs for the development of the policy framework and strategy for post-basic education in Madagascar. It identifies and addresses the constraints in re-orienting the post-basic education and training system towards meeting medium-term labor market needs, supporting growth in both the formal and informal sectors of the economy and the longer-term development needs of the country.

The transformation of education is a pillar of the Madagascar Action Plan (MAP), the second-generation poverty reduction strategy plan of the Government of Madagascar (GOM), covering the period 2007–11. Consistent with this goal, the President announced a major re-structuring of school education in 2005. The reform of primary education and junior secondary education (JSE), which will be launched in 2008, is detailed in the new Education for All (EFA) Plan prepared by the Ministry of National Education (*Ministère de l'Education Nationale*— MEN), covering the period 2008–11. The EFA Plan (MEN, 2008a) was endorsed by the education partners in February 2008 and has received funding support from the Education for All-Fast Track Initiative (EFA-FTI) global partnership. While concentrating its efforts on preparing the reform of basic education, the MEN simultaneously began preparatory work to design the reform of post-basic education. This study was designed to assist the MEN in this process.

The study incorporates analysis and findings of eleven background papers commissioned by the World Bank, the MEN and *Agence Francaise de Développement* (AFD). The complete list is given in the references.

Ambitions of the MAP and an Education System in Crisis

The MAP envisages a structural change in the economy of Madagascar and lays out ambitious targets for growth, investment, and exports. Whether they can be realized in their entirety or not, the orientation of the MAP is to significantly increase domestic and foreign investment and recent trends suggest an upturn in the latter. If successful, the implementation of the MAP will change the demand for skills and knowledge in fundamental ways. First, the sectoral/regional composition of new jobs will change as the priority sectors identified in the MAP grow. Second, as new technology is introduced, the skills content of jobs will increase. Third, the adaptation of technology to local needs will require trained specialists and research workers.

The education and training system will affect all the other pillars of the MAP (see Figure 1). Education and training can contribute to growth in Madagascar by (i) providing more human capital, specifically the skills and knowledge that current and new workers need to work productively, and (ii) increasing the stock of business and technological knowledge used in production. Technological knowledge is here used in the broad economic sense as comprising feasible ways to produce desired goods and services from available inputs, and includes scientific and managerial knowledge and practices that may have been created and applied elsewhere. These two factors are distinct though, in practice, complementary and both complement investment in physical capital. Firms can also augment human capital and technological knowledge through training and research and development; in many countries, however, this is only possible through collaboration with education and training institutions.

Madagascar's education indicators show how far the education system is from playing the required role in supporting growth. The primary completion rate increased rapidly from

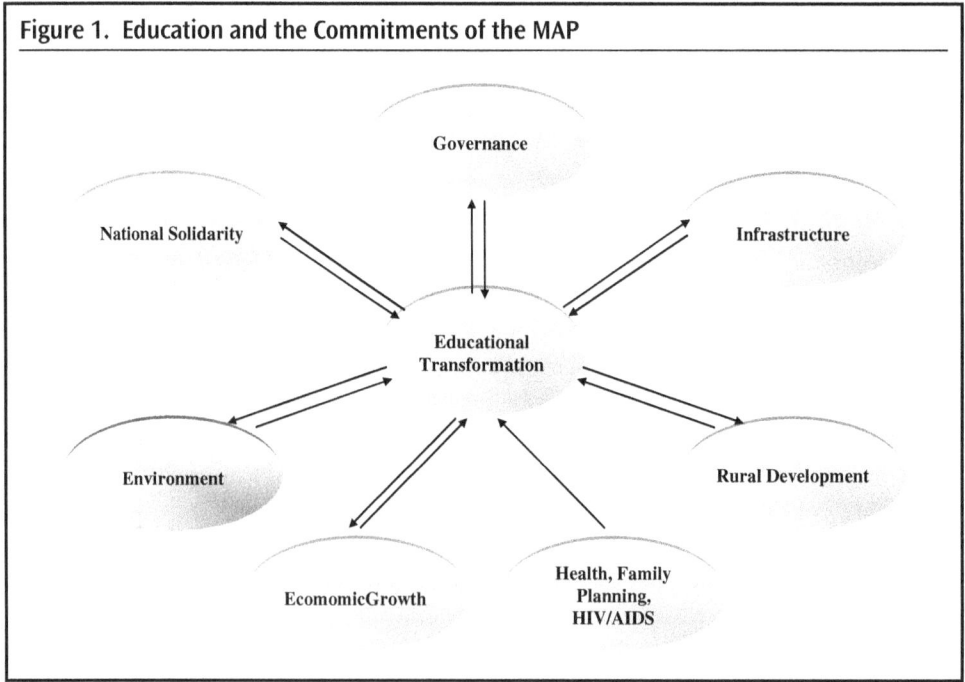

Figure 1. Education and the Commitments of the MAP

below 35 percent in 2002/03, but in 2006/07, it was still under 60 percent. The gross enrollment ratio (GER) in 2006/07 was only 32 percent in Junior Secondary Education (JSE) and around 10 percent in Senior Secondary Education (SSE). These figures are lower than the SSA averages of 30 percent and 13 percent, respectively. Only two percent of university age students are enrolled in universities—one of the lowest participation rates in the world.

Additional data provides further evidence that Madagascar's post-basic education system is in crisis. Out of the approximately 900 university faculty member, only 2 percent (16 people) are under 40 years, 92 percent are over 45 years, and 31 percent are 55 or older. Faculty publication rates are very low, with most not publishing anything over the last three years. In 2005, just one percent of the faculty published in journals tracked in the ISI Web of Science by ten scholars. Moreover, there has been no major curriculum reform for decades. University level education operates within the framework of an antiquated francophone model, 10 years after France and the majority of European countries started moving to the three tier system of bachelor's, master's and doctoral level programs.

The envisaged reform of basic education, comprising primary and junior secondary education, is the first major reform of the system since independence. It builds on the successes of increasing primary enrollment and completion since 2003, when fees for primary education were abolished. Primary education will be re-structured from 5 to 7 years, and junior secondary education will be changed from grades 6–8 to grades 8–10. The government's targets are to ensure that all children complete 5 years of primary education and 65 percent of children complete 7 years of education by 2015. Junior secondary education will be gradually expanded. The lengthening of the primary cycle and the move towards a basic education cycle of 10 years are consistent with international trends to ensure that children receive an adequate foundation of knowledge and skills for the future.

Policy Dilemmas in Post-basic Education and a Window of Opportunity

Madagascar's education system has operated in a policy vacuum for a long time. Each new government, and sometimes each new Minister, has introduced *ad hoc* changes or initiatives, leaving the basic system untouched. Sometimes these changes have added to the problems. Figure 2 shows how enrollments in higher education have been affected by government directives. Enrollment expanded dramatically in the 1980s, to an average of 35,000, with an equally dramatic fall in the 1990s to about 22,000. This decline was due to drastic measures adopted by the government to regulate enrollment, including the elimination of make-up session for the *baccalauréat* examination and changes to student scholarship policies. After 2003, enrollments started increasing again, regaining the level of two decades ago. Similarly, this increase in enrollment was due to more liberal policies on access and student scholarships. Small-scale initiatives to increase enrollment were introduced from 2000 onwards, in a limited number of universities and TVET institutions.[1] Nonetheless, there was no overall policy goal for the development of higher education.

Currently, the main pressure is to increase access and enrollment at the post-basic level. This pressure is generated by the internal dynamics of population growth and basic education reform. Specifically, demographic growth and the increasing numbers of primary school completers are generating strong private demand for secondary education. Further, because it will take time to achieve universal completion of primary education, there will continue to be a

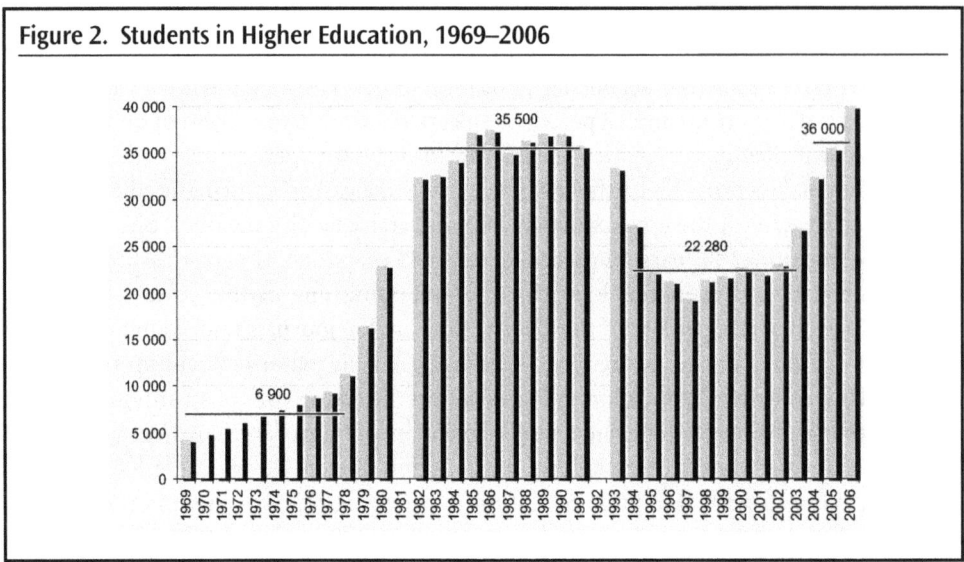

Note: Excludes students enrolled in distance education.
Source: Zaafrane (2008) analysis of MEN data.

large pool of primary school leavers who not only do not gain access to formal post-primary education, but also do not have the literacy and numeracy skills to compete in the labor market or to become effective members of society. Hence, alternative avenues to post-primary skill development, outside the formal education system, will be needed. While the government cannot be impervious to increasing social and political pressures on this count, it will be important to improve educational quality before massively scaling up access. There is little point in scaling up access when educational quality remains poor. Doing so could also be detrimental, both socially and economically. Further, improvements in quality could also increase the supply of places, by reducing repetition and the time taken to complete a cycle.

The reform of primary and junior secondary education creates another set of internal pressures for reform. First, post-basic education reform must ensure continuity in the curriculum across education cycles. Plans for basic education reform include reform of primary and junior secondary curriculum to focus on core knowledge and skill acquisition (Figure 3). Curriculum reform is complemented by changes to teacher training that will focus on active, participatory teaching methods.

Second, the expansion of primary education and junior secondary education demands large number of new, higher quality teachers. This need can be met only by reforms at the tertiary level, to train a larger number of teachers and to teach effective teaching methods.

The external pressure from economic changes and international trends in education is primarily on another front—to upgrade quality and the content and process of education, so that graduates have the skills required by the labor market and the education system can generate and adapt knowledge required by the economy. As Madagascar's economy integrates into regional and global trade—it is a member of the South African Development Community (SADC)—the pressures from employers and from the labor market will increase. The problem is that the education and training system in Madagascar is still largely insulated from these external pressures, due to its governance and financing mechanisms

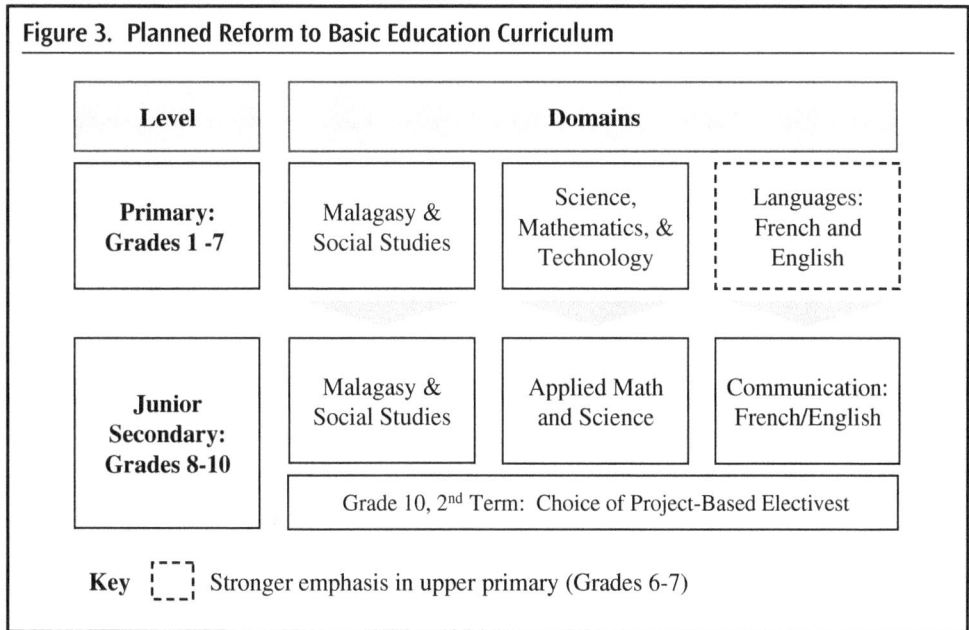

Figure 3. Planned Reform to Basic Education Curriculum

and the absence of a policy that links education development to economic and social development. A deliberate policy, backed up by appropriate instruments, is required to make the education system more outward oriented and more accountable for its performance.

Finally, resources are limited and will continue to be so over the medium-term. The economy has recovered from the 2002 political crisis. The MAP projects an increase in the growth rate to 7–12 percent per annum, substantially higher than the historical 3.5 percent average annual growth realized during the period 1996–2006. It also projects an increase in internal revenue generation to about 14 percent of GDP, from the historical average of 11 percent. Even if these targets are realized and the government allocates 25 percent of its budget to education (as stated in the EFA plan), resources will be well below "needs." This will be especially critical for the post-basic education, given the priority for primary education.

Hence, the challenge is to manage the unavoidable pressures to expand the post-basic education system while upgrading its quality and changing its orientation, which is the real necessity. This can be done by seeking new solutions to the problems of investing in quality improvement and expanding access.

The next few years provide a window of opportunity for the post-basic education system to put in place the reforms required to respond to these pressures. They should be firmly in place by 2011, when the surge of primary education and junior secondary education completers will begin to be felt, if the reforms at those levels are successfully implemented.

Lessons Learned from Basic Education Reform

As noted earlier, Madagascar is undertaking major reform of its basic education system. Changes have been underway since 2003, and will be largely completed by 2011. The reform has been widely recognized for its progress thus far, and several lessons can be applied to post-basic reform.

First, the implementation of reforms beyond the primary level is best done through their voluntary adoption by individual institutions, encouraged by incentives and technical support, rather than through launching system wide changes in one go. This is best exemplified by the proposed reform of junior secondary education, where the strategy is to introduce new "*collèges d'excellence*" that are networked with existing schools. Existing schools gradually adopt new curriculum and teaching methods with the guidance of the *collèges d'excellence*. Complicated reforms with too many elements are difficult to manage, especially in a low capacity environment.

Second, reforms focusing on improving quality and relevance need to cover an entire package—curriculum, teachers, learning materials, financing and management—if they are to bring about desired changes in the classroom. Major cost reductions can be realized through curriculum re-organization, utilizing teachers and classrooms more effectively. Careful planning and realistic phasing are important.

Finally, basic education reform has enjoyed tremendous ownership and leadership by the Ministry. High-level leadership and broad-based political ownership are both critical to the success of post-basic education reform.

Content and Structure of the Report

This study makes a contribution to the development of a coherent strategy for post-basic education. It presents findings and suggests priorities for reform, structured around three broad topics: (i) improving the quality and relevance of the post-basic education and training system, with a focus on skill development and knowledge transfer/creation in a changing economic environment; (ii) identifying cost-effective measures for increasing access to post-basic education, including greater equity in participation; and (iii) proposing key reforms in governance, financing and management, to enable the post-basic education and training system to respond to external changes and shape the future.

Chapters 2 and 3 analyze the current status in enrollment trends and completion rates in post-basic education and education and labor market linkages, respectively. Chapter 4 presents the issues and priority actions to improve quality and relevance, focusing on changes in desired outcomes, the curriculum structure and duration of cycles, teachers and learning materials in each sub-sector. Chapter 5 presents options for increasing access and equity in a sustainable manner. Chapter 6 describes the degree to which the education system and firm-based training initiatives contribute to growth, and how they could be modified to become stronger drivers of growth in the future. Chapters 7 and 8 present findings relating to costs and governance, respectively, indicating the main reforms in financing, management and governance that are required. Chapter 9 concludes the report, reviewing the report's findings and outlining the reforms implied by the report's analysis.

CHAPTER 2

Trends in Enrollment and Completion

Enrollment Trends[2]

Madagascar has made impressive strides in primary enrollment, but enrollments at other levels are still low. Primary enrollment more than doubled between 1997 and 2006/07, with over 3.8 million students. About half a million children joined in 2003/04, after the abolition of primary school fees (Figure 4a). Since 2002, the growth in junior secondary and senior secondary has also been very rapid, growing at an annual rate of 16 and 12 percent, respectively (Figures 4b and 4c). The 1997–2007 growth rates for JSE and SSE are 11 percent and 9 percent respectively. Total enrollment in secondary education was only about 890,000 students (660,000 in JSE and 128,000 in SSE). While enrollments have increased in TVET and higher education, total enrollment is still relatively small: about 53,000 students in TVET and 58,000 in higher education.[3]

Population coverage at the post-basic levels of education is extremely low by international and SSA standards, and has hardly increased in last decade. The GER in secondary education (junior and senior) was about 24 percent in 2006–7. This compares with about 50 percent in South Asia and over 70 percent in most other regions (Figure 5). Mauritius and Botswana, two middle income countries in SADC, have a secondary GER of approximately 90 and 75 percent, respectively. Madagascar's junior secondary GER which grew very slowly between 1996 and 2000 increased rapidly thereafter from about 20 percent to 32 percent in 2006/07. Coverage at the senior secondary level was stable at 5 percent

---

2. Enrollment data are based on the existing structure of education, comprising 5 years of primary, 4 years of junior secondary and 3 years of senior secondary. Enrollment in TVET here refers to the school level, which starts after the primary cycle and covers the vocational centers and technical schools.
3. While the number of private TVET institutions is known, enrollment data are not available.

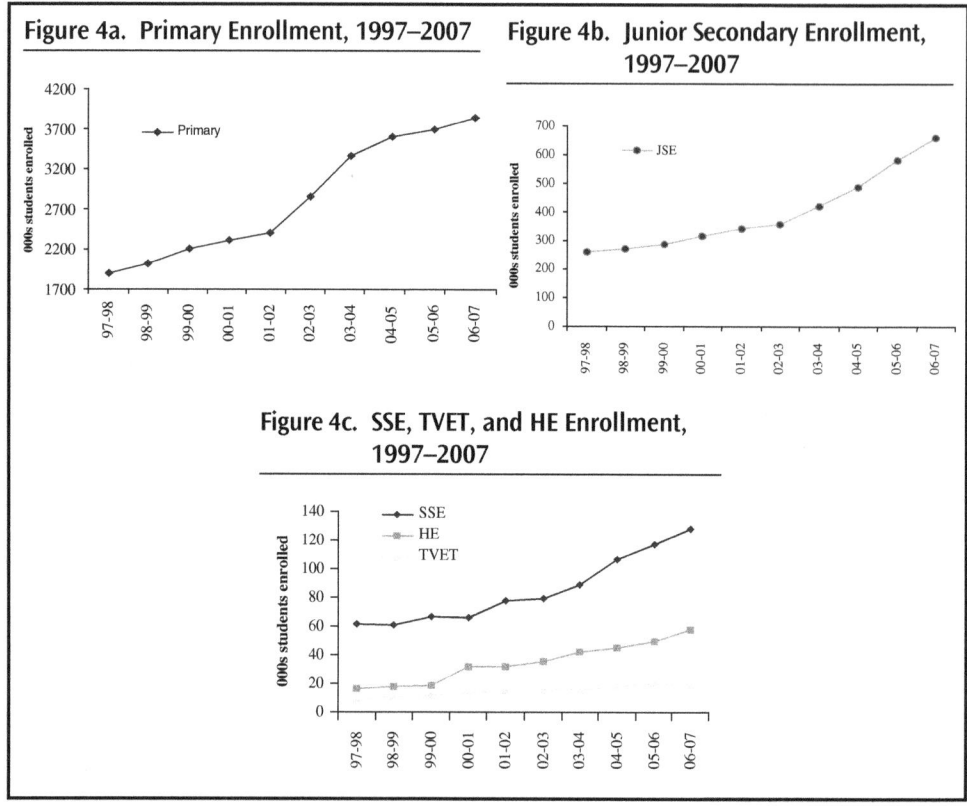

Source: MEN, administrative data.

before 2000 and is still below 10 percent. In higher education, the gross enrollment rate was about 2.5 percent. The number of students per 100,000 population was about 264. By comparison, the value of this indicator for SSA countries was 334 in 2005, and 435 for Anglophone SSA countries.

The private sector has contributed significantly to the expansion of secondary education. Both in junior and senior secondary, over 40 percent of enrollment has been in private institutions. In 2006/07, private senior secondary schools enrolled more than half the students. According to the most recent registration, private TVET institutions of all types enrolled 34,250 students in 350 institutions, or about two thirds of total enrollment. By contrast, the private sector share in higher education was less than 10 percent, having risen rapidly from a negligible share at the beginning of the decade (Figure 6).

Internal Efficiency and Transition Between Cycles

Dropout levels are high within and at the end of each school cycle. About half the children who enroll in grade 1 leave without completing the primary cycle, for public and private institutions combined. Clearly, ensuring universal completion of primary education is the main way to increase enrollment at higher levels. Despite increases in enrollment, the reduction in the dropout rate has been relatively low and constitutes one of the main

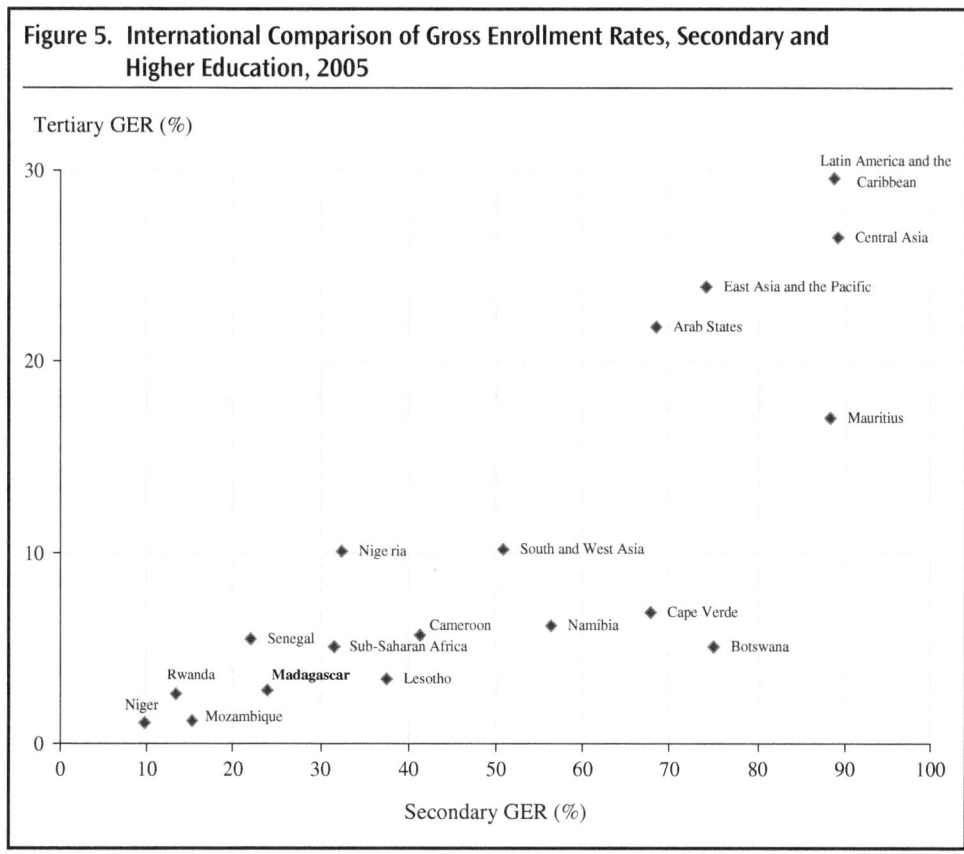

Figure 5. International Comparison of Gross Enrollment Rates, Secondary and Higher Education, 2005

Source: 1. UNESCO Institute for Statistics (http://stats.uis.unesco.org). 2. World Bank EdStats (http://sima.worldbank.org/edstats/)

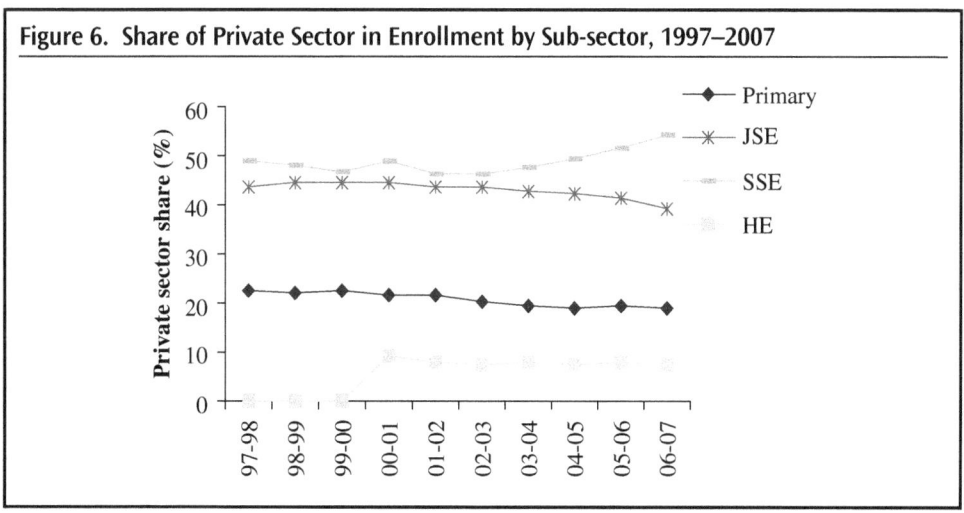

Figure 6. Share of Private Sector in Enrollment by Sub-sector, 1997–2007

Notes: See Annex Table 1.
Source: MEN, administrative data.

policy priorities in primary education, reflected in the new EFA plan. Only two-thirds of grade 5 children who appear in the end of cycle examination get the primary school leaving certificate.

The transition rate to JSE for primary completers is relatively high. About 70 percent of children who get the primary certificate enter junior secondary education.

About 4 out of 10 students who enter grade 6 (first year of JSE) dropout during the four year cycle. This indicator has not improved significantly in the period 2000–2006. About 60 percent of those who sit for the junior secondary final examination do not pass. Student retention within the senior secondary level is higher, with almost 85 percent of students who enter in grade 9 reaching grade 12. This partly reflects the high degree of selectivity at the senior secondary stage.

A similar situation prevails in TVET. In the first year of study in LTPs (senior secondary), about one-third of students drops out (27.2 percent and 35.2 per cent, in 2002–03 and 2003–04, respectively). Vocational training centers exhibit similar wastage: 30 percent of students dropped out after the first year of training in 2002–03, 19 percent in 2003–04.

Less than 45 percent of grade 12 students pass the *baccalauréat* after senior secondary education and about half of those who pass enter tertiary education. The pass rate in the *baccalauréat* examination has improved from about 30 percent in early part of the decade. Not all students who pass the *baccalauréat* enter the university—this is a significant departure from the French system, where *baccalauréat* holders, by law, are entitled to enter university. In Madagascar, approximately 54 percent of those who pass the *baccalauréat* entered tertiary education in 2005–06. There are differences in the entry rates into higher education, depending on the option chosen in senior secondary education. In the academic series, tertiary education entry rates are very high in mathematics (95 percent), science (80 percent). By contrast, only 45 percent of those who pass the *baccalauréat* in the arts series ("*Lettres*") enter tertiary education. The technical series, which enroll less than 15 percent of SSE students, have lower entry rates, partly because more students take up jobs after passing the examination (Figure 7).

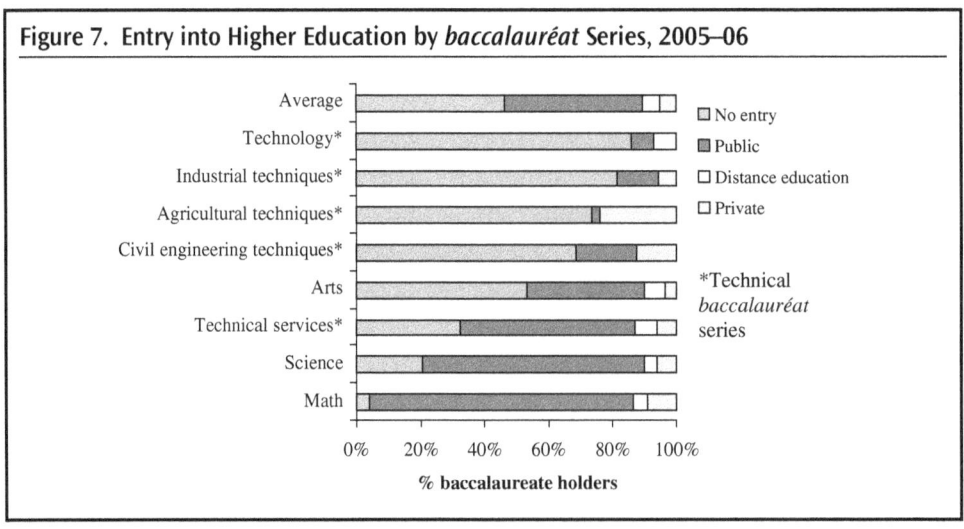

Figure 7. Entry into Higher Education by *baccalauréat* Series, 2005–06

Source: Zaafrane (2008) analysis of MEN data.

Nearly 40 percent of students who enter university education dropped out after the first year in 2004–05, for public and private institutions combined. The drop-out rate has been as high as 70 percent in some years, and is largely due to the high failure rate on 1st year examinations (close to 50 percent). It means that students lose a year and leave without any additional qualification beyond the *baccalauréat*.

The high dropout rate is due to both internal and external factors—including overcrowded classes, inconsistent disbursement of external scholarships, or lack of student clarity about their professional ambitions, and other socio-economic causes. Whether driven by internal or external factors, the high dropout rate represents an enormous waste of resources for both universities and students.

There are also significant variations across universities. Effectively, the first year of tertiary education represents another selection mechanism after the *baccalauréat* and means that only 30 percent of *baccalauréat* candidates really continue into tertiary education (Figure 8).

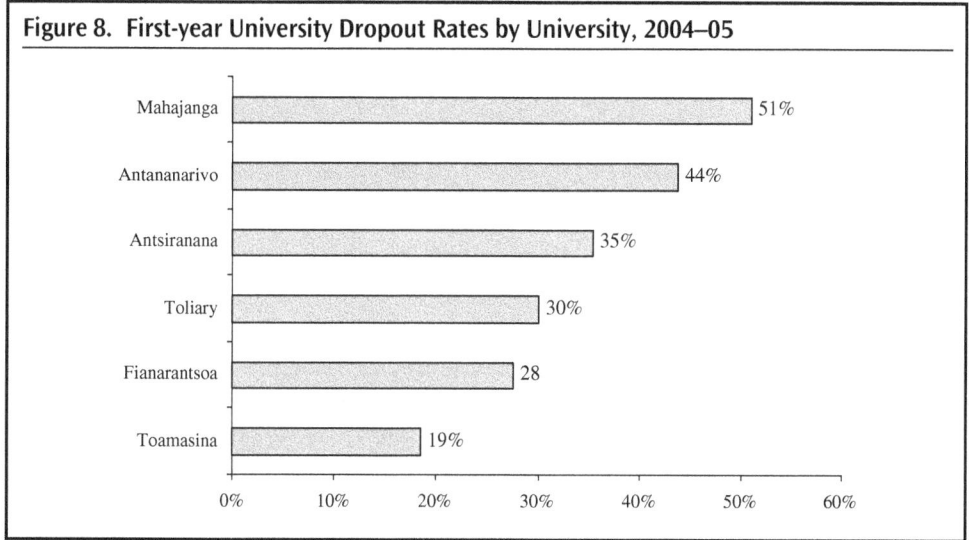

Figure 8. First-year University Dropout Rates by University, 2004–05

- Mahajanga: 51%
- Antananarivo: 44%
- Antsiranana: 35%
- Toliary: 30%
- Fianarantsoa: 28
- Toamasina: 19%

Source: MEN data, Zaafrane (2008) analysis.

Significantly, the first year dropout rate is much lower in the short-duration courses of non-university institutions. Compared to a dropout rate of 15 percent in the short-duration courses, the dropout rate in the long duration courses is 38 percent. This is related to the superior pass rate for end-of-year exams in short-duration courses, where 70–90 percent of students pass the first year. By contrast, low pass rates in university long-duration courses contribute to high dropout rates. The dropout rate is especially high in the sciences, at 49 percent, while in the arts it is 41 percent. In medicine, examinations at the end of the first year contribute to a close to 60 percent dropout rate.

Such high levels of dropout, especially in the first year, despite the rather stringent selection mechanisms in place, indicate inadequate preparation for the course of study, or student interest. In either case, there is a gross wastage of resources.

Pass rates on national examinations in TVET were about 70 percent for the junior secondary vocational training certificate (BEP) and 53 percent for the senior secondary technological *baccalauréat*. In 2005, there were significant differences across regions, with pass rates ranging from 29 percent to 70 percent.

Repetition rates are also very high and represent another source of wastage. This is another feature common to francophone systems, where repetition is used both as a pedagogical method and as a method of selection. The average repetition rate in junior secondary education was 10 percent and 14 percent in senior secondary education in 2005. Repetition rates are typically high in the first year and final year of the cycle, reflecting students re-taking courses to pass the final examination. For example, the repetition rates in grade 9 (last year of junior secondary) and in grade 12 were 21 percent each. In TVET, the repetition rates ranged from 22 to 62 percent in senior secondary technical/vocational schools (*Lycées Technique Professionelle*-LTP) and 12–25 percent in junior secondary vocational training schools (*Centre de Formation Professionnelle*—CFP). In tertiary education, the repetition rate was about 14 percent in the long duration courses and 2–3 percent in the short-duration courses.

Internationally, there is no evidence that repetition improves learning outcomes. On the other hand, repetition can encourage dropout, especially for poor students who are unable to bear the cost of an additional year of schooling. Many countries, including France, have made systematic efforts to eliminate repetition in the school cycle, either through administrative measures or through changes in pedagogical practices.

Taken together, the high dropout and repetition rates indicate a very high level of inefficiency that a country with limited resources can ill afford.

Graduates

The cumulative effect of high dropout, repetition and failure is the very small number of graduates from each level. At the apex of the education system, tertiary education produced about 4,200 graduates in 2006, of which 2,351 had bachelor's degrees and another 1,000 had master's degrees. There were only 380 graduates beyond that level in university education. About 25,000 students passed the *baccalauréat* and 41,000 passed the junior secondary certificate.[4]

Figure 9 shows that a significant proportion of those who enter are not able to continue through. The high failure rates in BEPC and the BAC and in completing higher education are responsible for this, though dropout within the cycle (due to failure on end of year examinations) also contributes.

Out-of-School Children and Youth

The corollary of the inefficient education system is a large number of out-of-school children and young adolescents with low levels of education. Household data show that in 2005 about 850,000 youth aged 11 to 18 years had dropped out of school after receiving some education and another 500,000 had never been to school.[5] Providing alternative, flexible learning oppor-

---

4. Zaafrane, 2008. Background studies to the *Rapport d'état sur le système éducatif national (RESEN) 2001 de Madagascar* (2001 Country Status Report on Education) drew similar conclusions.

5. This age group corresponds to the theoretical age group for junior and senior secondary education in Madagascar.

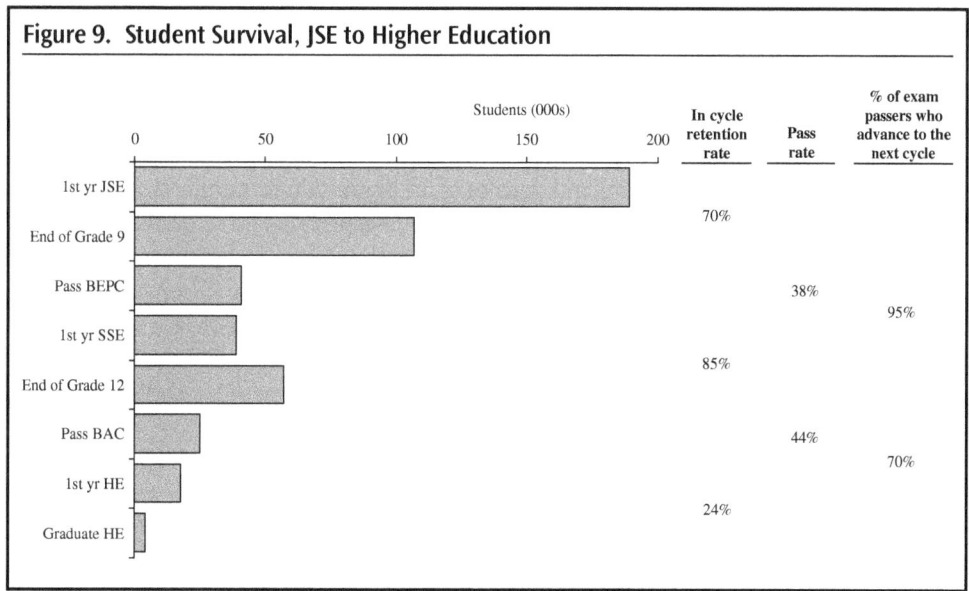

Figure 9. Student Survival, JSE to Higher Education

Notes: 1. In-cycle retention rates are calculated using a semi-longitudinal method and excluding repeaters. See MEN 2008b. 2. '% of exam passers who advance to the next cycle' is calculated as the number of children who enroll in the first year of a cycle divided by the number of children who have passed the qualifying exam at the end of the previous cycle.
Source: MEN, 2008b, in progress; Zaafrane, 2008; and World Bank 2008.

tunities for some of these children would help to raise the educational attainment of youth. The breakdown of this group by age and education level would enable the design of targeted interventions. Specifically, about quarter of a million children in the age group 11–15 years had no education; possibly, the only realistic approach for this group would be to provide community-based basic literacy programs, if resources permitted. Another 220,000 children had not completed primary education and could be targeted for primary completion. About 61,000 had completed primary education and could therefore be enrolled in post-primary courses. In the older age group (16–18 years), about 250,000 youth had no education, 330,000 youth had some primary education and 176,000 had completed primary education. The latter group could conceivably be targeted for completing primary level courses combined with skills training for the labor market. A differentiated approach for these different sub-groups would be better than providing uniform programs delivering basic literacy skills to all.

Equity

Regional disparities in access and completion are pronounced, and they start at the primary level. About 30 districts have primary completion rates that are below 30 percent and these are mostly in the coastal and southern areas. There are parts of Madagascar where the supply of junior and senior secondary graduates is insufficient to meet the demand for primary/junior secondary school teachers, perpetuating low educational attainment.

Inequality in access and completion is very high beyond the primary level. Only 9 percent of children from the lowest income quintile reached lower secondary education, and only 1 percent reached senior secondary education in 2005 (World Bank 2008). As Figure 10 indicates, post-primary education is virtually the preserve of the richest segments. The figure shows the educational attainment of the population by quintile level in 2004, reflecting the cumulative effect of investment in education over several generations. About 10 percent of the richest quintile had higher education and another 23 percent secondary education. At the other end of the spectrum, less than 1 percent of the poorest three quintiles (hence, 60 percent of the population) had tertiary education, and only 3–8 percent had secondary education.

The disparities in educational attainment between the richest and poorest quintiles are caused by a shortage in public secondary school places, where fees are lowest, and the concentration of public secondary schools in urban areas; the direct cost of secondary education in private schools, which is prohibitive for many poor families; and the opportunity cost of enrollment for poor children, especially as children grow older and if they must repeat years in school.

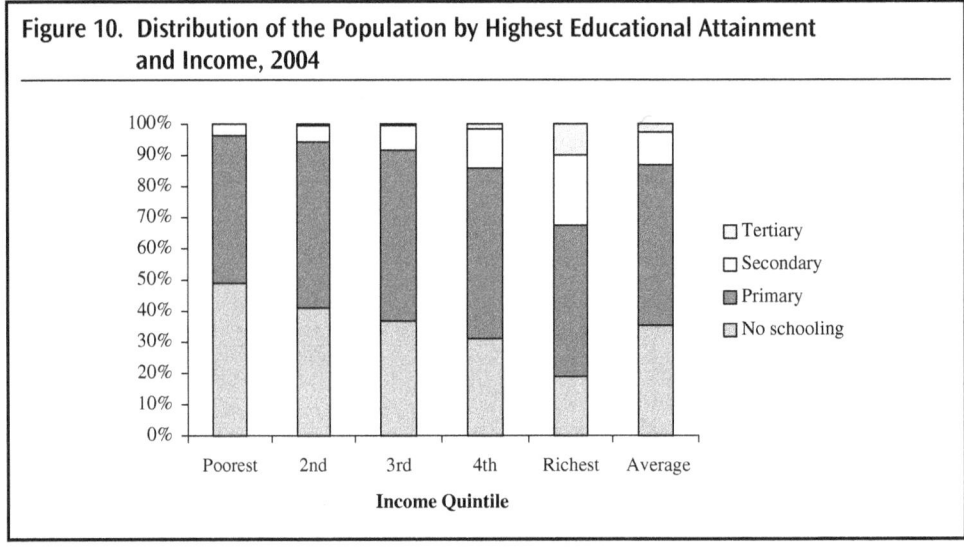

Figure 10. Distribution of the Population by Highest Educational Attainment and Income, 2004

Source: INSTAT, DSM, and Enquête Prioritaire auprès des Ménages, 2004.

Data on current enrollment rates show a marked improvement in the participation of poor children in primary education and some improvement in junior secondary education. However, there has been virtually no change in senior secondary education. For the lowest quintile, the net enrollment rate increased from 45 percent to 71 percent between 2001 and 2005. In the top quintile, there is universal enrollment. In JSE, the enrollment rates for the bottom three quintiles were 9, 11, and 18 respectively in 2005. These had risen from 1, 3, and 8, respectively in 2001. The enrollment rate in SSE amongst the poorest income groups was between 1 and 2 percent in 2005, reflecting no change over the period.

Undoubtedly, equity at higher levels will increase as more children complete primary education. However, this will take a long time if the normal selection mechanisms of the education system continue to operate. If Madagascar wishes to rapidly improve the participation of poorer children in post-basic education, targeted interventions will be required to offset the direct and indirect costs of education for the poor and to bring the supply of schools closer to the rural population.

Table 1. Madagascar–Net Enrollment Rates per Income Level in 2001 and 2005 (%)								
		Quintile					Madagascar	
Level	Year	I	II	III	IV	V	Ratio Q5:Q1	Total
Primary	2001	45	56	62	76	85	1.9	62
	2005	71	79	84	92	99	1.4	83
JSE	2001	1	3	8	15	44	44.0	12
	2005	9	11	18	22	38	4.2	19
SSE	2001	1	0	2	3	14	14.0	4
	2005	1	1	2	6	14	14.0	4

Source: Enquêtes Prioritaires auprès des Ménages 2001 and 2005.

Conclusion

Madagascar's education system suffers from serious inefficiencies, while participation in post-basic education is extremely inequitable. These issues require supply side interventions, to improve the distribution of schools, but also to reduce repetition and dropout. The latter are linked to pedagogical methods as well. They may also require demand side interventions to enable children from poor families to participate in post-basic education.

CHAPTER 3

Education-Labor Market Linkages

Education and training contribute to economic growth in two critical ways. They can raise the stock of human capital and, hence, labor productivity and increase the stock of scientific/technological knowledge applied to productive uses. Many factors, such as health, nutrition and education, contribute to human capital. However, education and training contribute most directly to the creation of skills and knowledge of the workforce and is often used as the proxy of human capital. Both pre-employment education and training (provided by schools, universities and training institutions) and post-education training provided to employees by firms are important. Clearly, the mere availability of a skilled and knowledgeable workforce is insufficient to raise growth; a favorable macroeconomic environment, functioning labor and credit markets and other factors are also necessary.

The growth strategies of the MAP will create new demands for skills and knowledge. As Madagascar's economy integrates with the global economy and trade increases, labor will be re-allocated, with new skills being required for employment in new industries or sectors and re-training of the labor force required in industries that will decline. Foreign direct investment (FDI) has increased rapidly in recent years. Between 2002 and 2005, FDI inflows rose from US$15 million to US$85 million; in 2006, the inflow rose to US$294 million and in 2007 to close to US$1 billion, or 13 percent of GDP.[6] Much of this FDI is in mining, but the government's policy is to attract investment in other sectors as well. Agricultural growth and regional development are key pillars of the MAP. Education and training can

---

6. Data for 2002 to 2005 are from the World Bank's World Development Indicator database and are net flows based on balance of payments data. For 2006 and 2007, the data are from the Central Bank of Madagascar.

play a key role in increasing labor productivity in agriculture and ensuring the more balanced distribution of a skilled labor force.

This chapter examines the stocks and flows of human capital in the labor force. The most widely used measure is the education attainment of the population or the labor force, as measured by the years of education. Although this is a crude measure of the skills, knowledge and competencies of the workforce, it provides a broad indication of the human capital base and enables comparison with other countries. The national analysis is complemented by an analysis of the distribution of human capital in different regions. The chapter also presents recent changes in the structure of employment and the labor market and how they have affected private rates of return to education. The two main sources of data are the 2005 household survey (*Enquête Prioritaire auprès des Ménages,* 2005) and the Investment Climate Assessment (ICA) Survey of 2005.

Labor Status of Population

Of the estimated 19.1 million people in Madagascar (2005), 9.17 million were of working age (15–64 years), 4.78 million were children aged 6–14 years and the remainder was either less than 6 or more than 65 years old. Although some children under the age of 15 also work, we restrict the labor force analysis to those between the ages of 15–64 years. Approximately 7.87 million were in employment; of the 1.3 million out of employment, 83 percent reported themselves as economically inactive. The labor force, comprising those in employment and those seeking work (unemployed), consisted of 8.08 million individuals, representing a rise of 11 percent over 2001. Open unemployment, as in many agricultural economies, is low at about 2.6 percent of the labor force (Figure 11).

The primary sector accounted for 80 percent of those in employment and services account for another 17 percent. The share of the industrial sector is miniscule (2.5 percent).

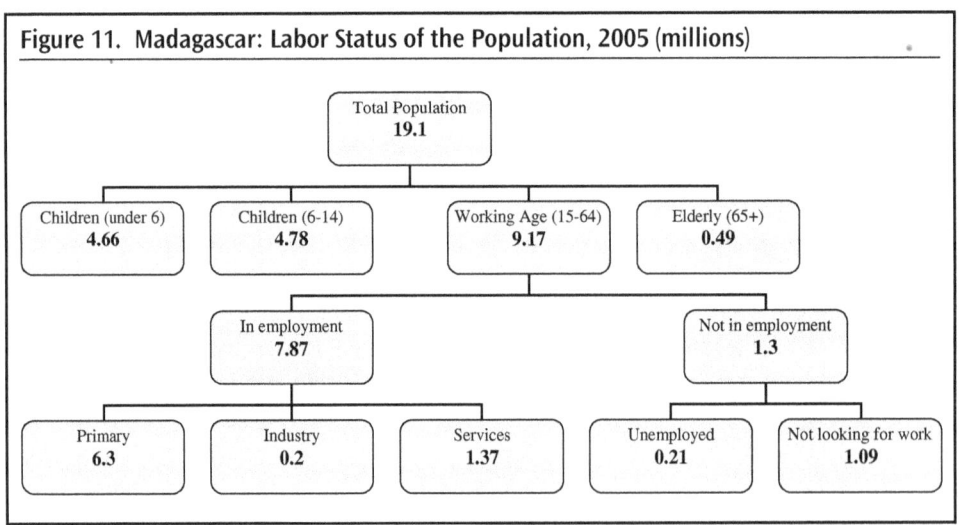

Figure 11. Madagascar: Labor Status of the Population, 2005 (millions)

Source: Adapted from Stifel et al (2007) analysis of *Enquête Prioritaire auprès des Ménages* 2005 data.

Between 2001 and 2005, employment in the primary sector increased by 1.2 million. Even its share in total employment rose from 72 percent. Employment in the industrial sector fell, driven by job losses in manufacturing, with a shift to agriculture.

Educational Attainment of the Population: Stocks and Flows

The human capital stock is proxied by the education level of the population aged 15 years or more. The following education levels have been used: (i) less than primary education (comprising those with no education and those that have not completed grade 5) (ii) primary education complete (iii) secondary education complete and (iv) and post-secondary education. (The highest education level attained is used to determine the percentage shares of the population).

Figure 12 shows the distribution of Madagascar's working age population (15–64 years old) by education level, and in comparison to the population aged 15 and above in low-income countries in South Asia. The base of the pyramid is wide in Madagascar, reflecting the large proportion of the population which has less than primary education. The pyramid tapers to a very narrow point, with only 1.7 percent of the age group having post-secondary education. As a country accumulates human capital, the middle level widens. This is shown by Sri Lanka where, by 2000, 50 percent of the population had secondary education. Madagascar's human capital distribution in 2005 approximates most closely that

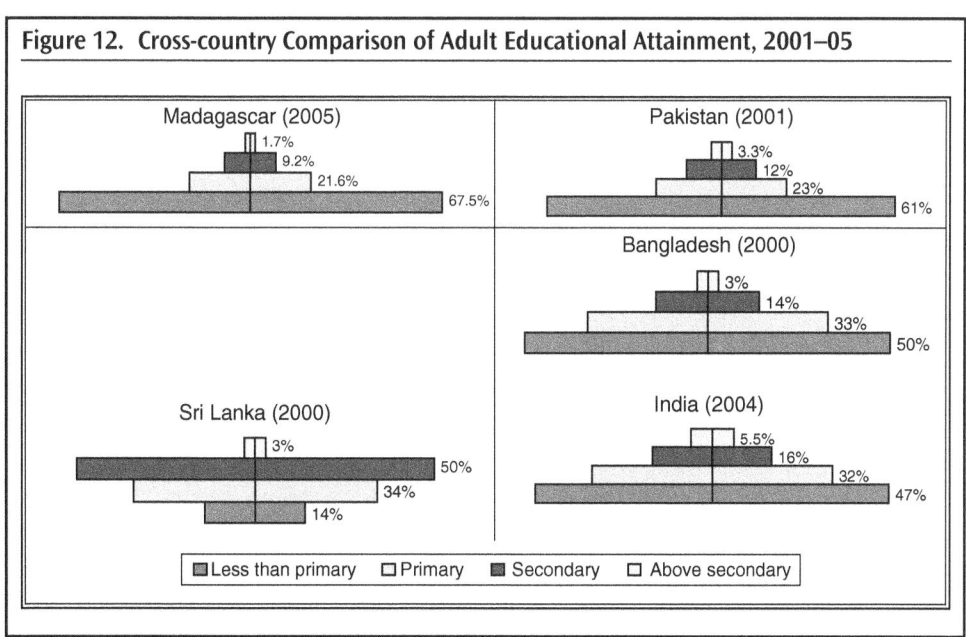

Figure 12. Cross-country Comparison of Adult Educational Attainment, 2001–05

Note: Madagascar data is population 15–64 years old; other countries' data is population 15 years and above. Data is for the following years: Madagascar—2005; Pakistan—2001; Bangladesh—2000; India—2004; and Sri Lanka—2000.
Sources: Madagascar: World Bank analysis of *Enquête Prioritaire auprès des Ménages* 2005 data. Other countries: Riboud et al., 2006.

of Pakistan in 2001, where over 60 percent of the population was illiterate. Equally noteworthy are the facts that even Pakistan has a higher share of the population with secondary and post-secondary education—and that Madagascar's current level of secondary attainment is comparable to that of Sri Lanka forty years ago (not shown in figure). In short, the educational attainment of Malagasy adults seriously lags that of other low income countries.

Madagascar has extremely low levels of educational attainment of the labor force and that of the younger age groups has been declining. The average years of education of the employed labor force remained constant at about 4 years between 2001 and 2005. The average years of education reflects cumulative investments in education. A striking feature of these data are that the human capital stock of the cohorts aged 20 years and more has actually declined in 2005 compared to 2001, reflecting the neglect of education over a period of several decades. One positive development is the slight increase in average years of education of the youngest cohort (15–19 years), by about 0.6 years in this period, which reflects the recent upswing in primary education enrollment (Figure 13).

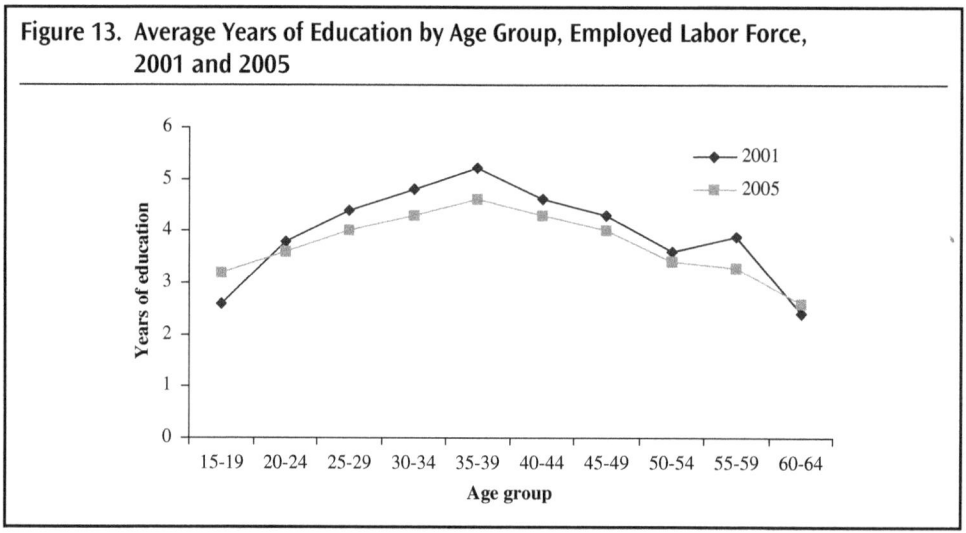

Figure 13. Average Years of Education by Age Group, Employed Labor Force, 2001 and 2005

Source: Adapted from Lassibille (2007) analysis of *Enquête Prioritaire* auprès des Ménages 2001 and 2005 data.

The proportion of young employed workers with less than primary education has increased, while the proportion with more than post primary education has declined (Figure 14). In 2001, 63 percent of the labor force under 30 years old had less than primary education (some primary or no education at all). In 2005, this proportion was 68 percent. This group must be considered functionally illiterate. The decline over time in attainment at higher levels of education is more striking and worrisome. The percentage of workers under 30 with senior secondary or higher education declined from 5 percent in 2001 to 3.7 percent in 2005. This trend must be reversed if Madagascar is to upgrade the skill level of its labor force.

Investment in human capital suffered a sharp setback from the 1970s to early 1980s, and Madagascar has to still re-gain this lost ground. Using the household survey data of

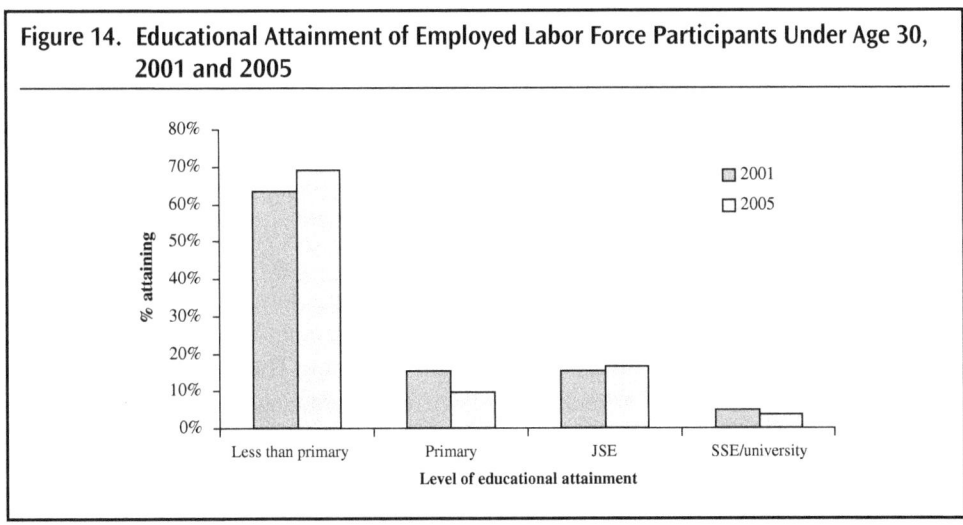

Figure 14. Educational Attainment of Employed Labor Force Participants Under Age 30, 2001 and 2005

Source: Adapted from Lassibille (2007) analysis of *Enquête Prioritaire* auprès des Ménages 2001 and 2005 data.

2005, we examine the educational attainment of different age groups. This gives an idea of investment over time: those aged 45–49 years in 2005 were born between 1955–60, while those aged 15–19 years in 2005 were born between 1985–90. For the oldest generation, born between 1940–45, the share of the population with at least grade 5 education attainment was 15 percent. This proportion peaked at 30 percent for the generation born in 1965–70. Thereafter, the proportion actually declined, resuming a slow growth only over the last 10 years. The grade 5 attainment of the youngest generation has only just surpassed what had been attained two decades ago. Moreover, there is no evidence as yet of any increase in the pace of investments—the slopes are roughly constant even during the periods of improvement (Figure 15).

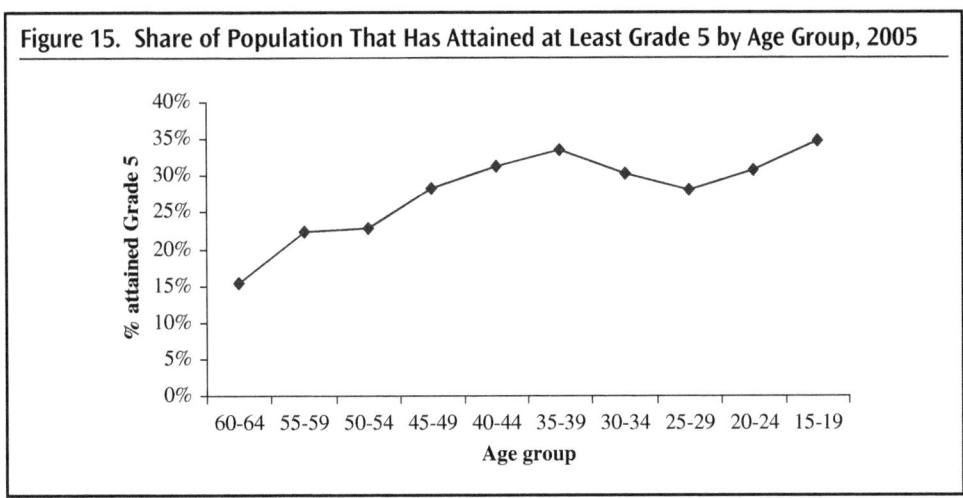

Figure 15. Share of Population That Has Attained at Least Grade 5 by Age Group, 2005

Source: World Bank analysis of *Enquête Prioritaire* auprès des Ménages 2005 data.

This stands in contrast with the trend in other regions, which also started with very low educational attainment a few decades ago. In South Asia, for example, the pace has clearly accelerated over the last two decades. Even a relatively poor performer such as Pakistan increased the proportion attaining grade 5 by 20 percentage points over the last two decades. Smaller countries, such as the Maldives and Bhutan, have made spectacular advances, the former reaching 90 percent grade 5 attainment in the same period.

Beyond primary education, the trend is alarming and shows that Madagascar has been disinvesting in post-primary education. About 14 percent of a generation had attained at least grade 9 (junior secondary) about 20 years ago, following a slow but steady increase over the preceding two decades. However, the most recent generation (20–24 year olds) has not regained that level after the steep decline in the 1980s and 1990s. The proportion of a cohort that had attained grade 12 had never exceeded 6 percent in Madagascar, but this had been halved for the most recent generation (Figures 16a and 16b).

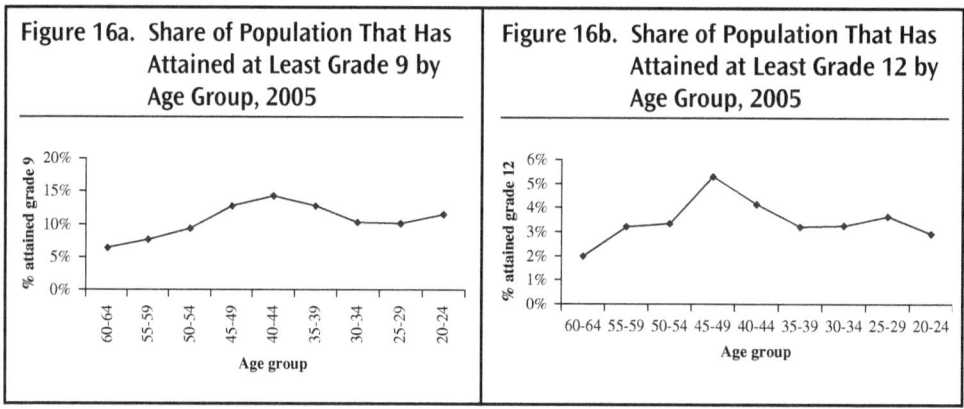

Source: World Bank analysis of *Enquête Prioritaire auprès des Ménages* 2005 data.

Figure 17 shows the stock of the employed labor force by highest educational/training qualification received and the estimated annual education and training awards in 2005. Many of those who receive an award will go on to receive higher awards and not all will join the labor force or employment. Therefore, the annual awards do not represent the flow of new entrants into the labor force. However, they can be used to assess the magnitude of new qualifications in relation to the existing skill distribution of employed persons. Awards of primary school and junior secondary certificates in 2005 represented only 14 and 8 percent of the stocks of employed persons who had these respective qualifications. New vocational training awards represented less than 2 percent of the employed labor force with this qualification (even though the stock itself is very small). In other words, the skills upgrading of the labor force at the base of the system is occurring at a very slow rate. On the other hand, the number of *baccalauréat*, bachelor's and master's level awards represented 18, 4 and 7 percent of the employed labor force with these respective qualifications. New awards represent a higher proportion of the employed persons with these qualifications because the number of the latter is so little. But it can also indicate that, for example, students try to obtain a master's qualification because the lower qualification (bachelor's degree) is not valued in the market.

The important policy issue is that the current situation does not result of conscious and strategic choices. It is the result of unmanaged student flows, the long duration of the post primary cycles and the irrelevance of qualifications, which forces students to continue with education. Madagascar would need to review these trends and set appropriate targets for student flows.

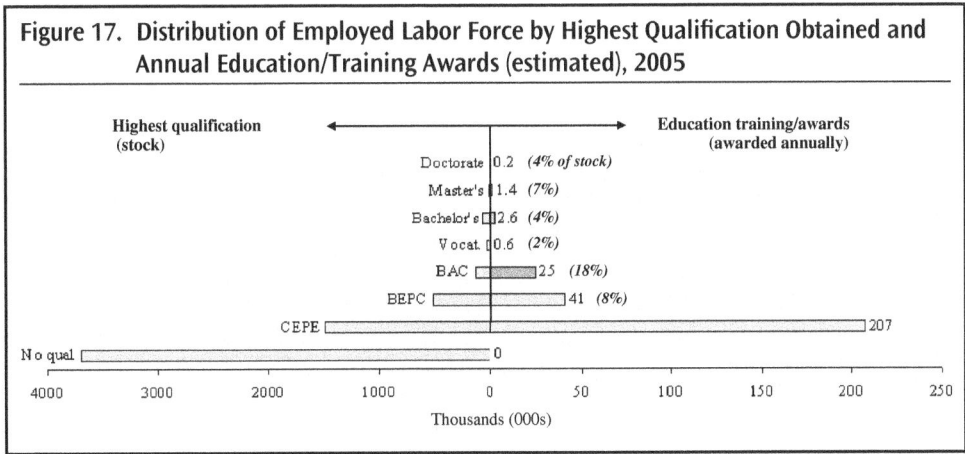

Figure 17. Distribution of Employed Labor Force by Highest Qualification Obtained and Annual Education/Training Awards (estimated), 2005

Source: World Bank analysis of *Enquête Prioritaire auprès des Ménages* 2005 data, MEN data.

Regional disparities in educational attainment are extremely large, and could impede the goal of promoting regional economic development. The region of Analamanga (near the capital Antananarivo) is the most educated. Five percent of the labor force had higher education, 41 percent had secondary education, and 12 percent had primary education. About 41 percent had less than primary education. At the other extreme, the region of Androy had 97 percent with less than primary education (53 percent with no education), only 2 percent with primary education, 4 percent with secondary education and 0.1 with higher education (Figure 18). As discussed in the previous chapter, educational disparities are strongly influenced by poverty. Analysis has also shown that low educational levels are strongly correlated with low population density.[7] Efforts to address regional disparities should therefore recognize the root causes of different levels of education and, as appropriate, develop policy measures to address them.

Regional variations in the sectoral distribution of employment are also quite pronounced. The proportion employed in the primary sector varies from 46 percent (Analamanga) to 96 percent (Androy). Industry is heavily concentrated in Analamanga, but even here it contributes only 8 percent of employment. In most regions, the share of industry is less than 0.5 percent. The regions with a high share of employment in agriculture are also those with a high share of people with less than primary education. These regions are characterized by a low skill equilibrium, where there is no incentive for individuals to

---

7. Lassibille, 2007. In CISCOs with primary completion rates of under 30%, population density is 18 people per km versus a national average of 200 people per km.

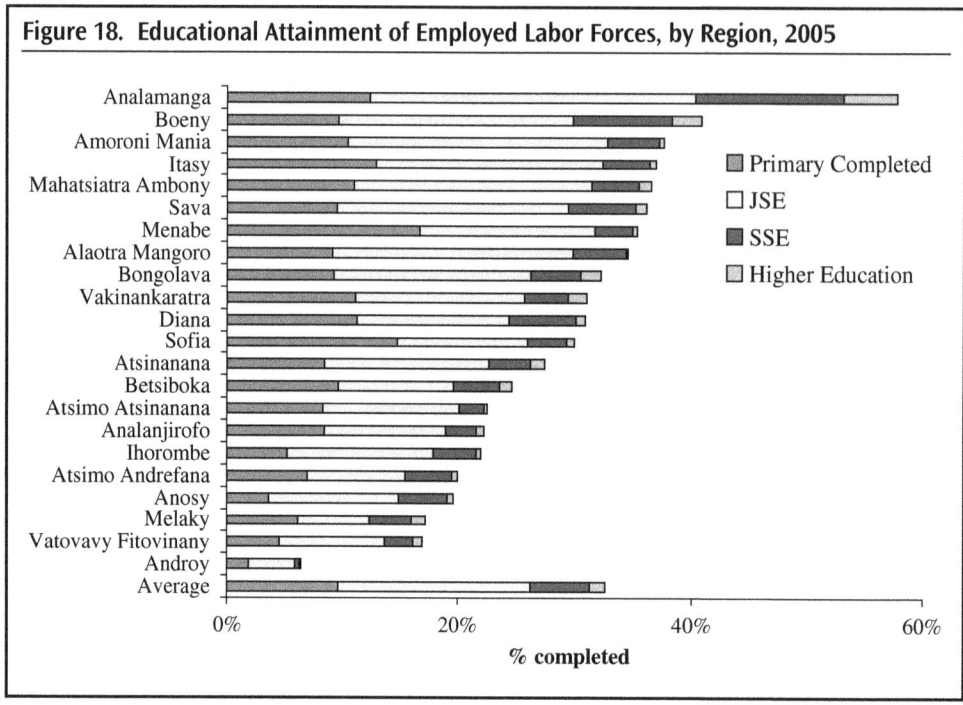

Source: Adapted from Lassibille (2007) analysis of *Enquête Prioritaire auprès des Ménages* 2005 data.

invest in education and no pressure for small scale producers in agriculture to upgrade productivity.

The MAP identifies some regions for targeted investment and growth in key sectors. These include: Diana in the north and Anosy in the south for tourism; Alaotra Mangoro and Menabe and Varinankaratra for agri-business, Anosy and Atsinanana for mining; and Analamanga for services and agro-industries. Apart from the latter, all of the others have between 4–7 percent of the labor force with more than senior secondary education and less than 2 percent with higher education (Figure 19).

Given Madagascar's size, the lack of transportation, housing and schooling facilities, normal labor market adjustments, such as internal migration, cannot correct these regional imbalances in the supply of skilled labor. Hence, even if the national supply were seemingly adequate at the aggregate level, it would be insufficient to support the country's regional development strategy. If the industry is capital intensive, with limited backward linkages, foreign investors can meet critical shortages of highly skilled labor through importing foreign workers. However, labor intensive sectors such as tourism and agri-business will need to depend on local labor if they are to be competitive.

Labor Market Changes and Returns to Investment in Education

Between 2001 and 2005, high quality jobs and wages declined, probably due to the crisis of 2002 and its after-effects. The share of wage and salary employees fell from 18.2 per-

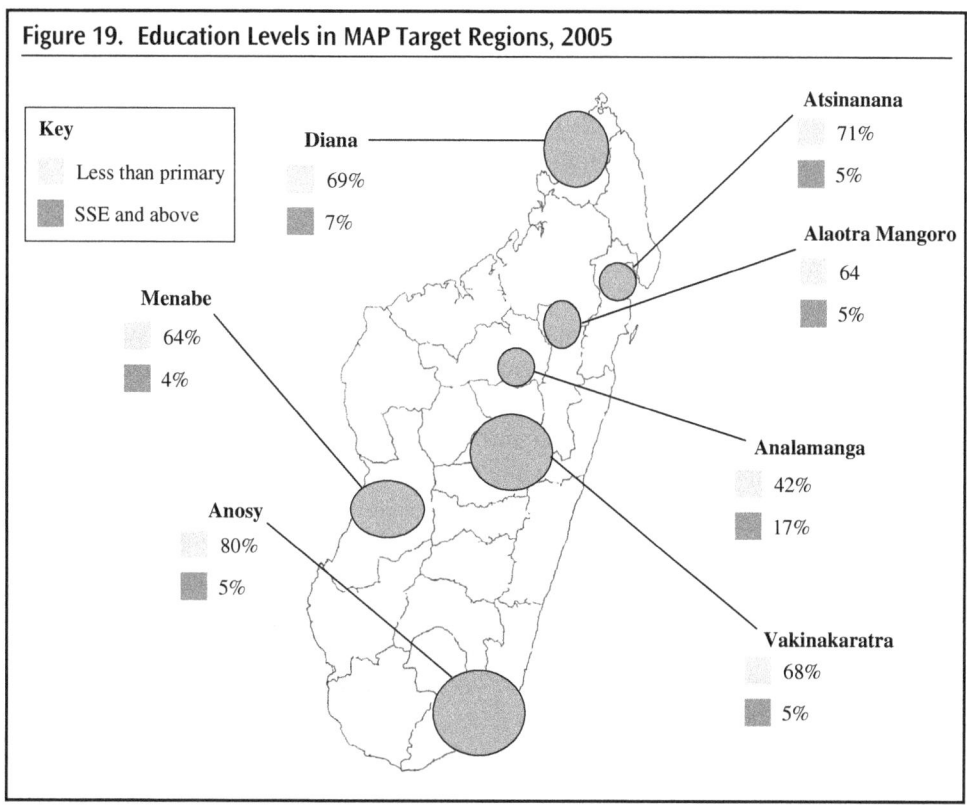

Figure 19. Education Levels in MAP Target Regions, 2005

Notes: MAP Key Regions from MEN. Education levels adapted.
Source: Adapted from Lassibille, 2007.

cent to 14.8 percent, with an absolute reduction in the number of jobs. The absolute loss of jobs among the highly skilled category was substantial—about 77,000 jobs, which resulted in about 40 percent reduction in the number of workers in this category. The majority of non-wage workers were employed in agriculture. Close to half the working population (48 percent) was classified as family helpers, a 10 percentage point increase over 2001.

The formal manufacturing sector seems to have rebounded after the crisis, but job creation trends indicate a major restructuring of manufacturing. Data from World Bank's Investment Climate Assessment survey (2005) shows that overall the net job creation between 2002 and 2004 was 20 percent. The survey covered 226 firms in the formal manufacturing sector. However, this represented partly a large rebound after the crisis of 2002. Job creation and losses varied widely across industrial sectors. There was a net loss of jobs in wood and furniture, paper, non-metallic and plastics. This was compensated by an increase of 21 percent in jobs in textiles, 13 percent in metallurgy and 11 percent in agro-industry and chemical products. Job creation was significantly higher in large enterprises, export oriented firms and those in export zones and foreign firms. By contrast, firms oriented to the domestic market created significantly fewer jobs (just over 6 percent) while public enterprises in the sample destroyed jobs (Lassibille, 2008).

Real wages of wage and salary earners in 2005 were one-third lower than in 2001.[8] However, there were significant differences by type of job. The wages of skilled and unskilled workers declined by 43 and 26 percent, respectively. Earnings of middle level professionals (*cadres moyens*) declined by about 83 percent. The highly skilled category (managers) saw their real earnings rise by 22 percent. Real earnings by level of education declined most substantially for those with secondary education (33 percent), compared to 6 percent for those with higher education. Regarding the latter, it seems that while real wages in higher skilled occupations rose, many of those who had had higher education were in occupation with lower earnings.

Nevertheless, disparities between wages and salaries at different levels of education continue to be high and have widened. In 2005, a person with higher education earned 2.4 times more than a person with secondary education. A person with secondary education got 1.9 times more than a person with primary education, while the differential between the latter and a person without any education was small (6 percent).

The overall rate of return to education for wage and salary earners declined but with substantial differences across levels of education. The rate of return in 2005 was estimated to be 6.4 percent in 2005, compared to 8.7 percent in 2001, reflecting the performance of the economy. The decline was very pronounced for primary and secondary education. The 6 additional years of investment in secondary education gave a private rate of return of just 5 percent in 2005, compared to 8 percent in 2001. Investment in junior secondary education gives a rate of return of just 1 percent.

Higher education has a very high rate of return which apparently increased between 2001 and 2005. The rate of return to higher education *increased* to 13 percent from 8 percent. In 2005, it was almost 50 percent higher than the rate of return for senior secondary education (8 percent) and 13 times higher than for someone with lower secondary education. These trends reflect the increase in relative salary differentials discussed earlier. The ICA survey for manufacturing firms in the formal sector shows an even higher rate (23 percent). Vocational and technical training have a higher rate of return (9.6 and 6.4 percent) compared to general secondary education (2 percent, see Figure 20).[9]

However, the analysis is limited by the fact that wage and salary earners constitute a relatively small proportion of the workforce. Education and training can also improve the productivity and earnings of workers in agriculture and the informal service sector. Given the huge numbers of those employed in these sectors, the effect on incomes and poverty reduction could also be substantial.

Skilled Labor Availability

The ICA survey also provided firms' perceptions about the most important constraints to growth. Lack of credit and its high cost and macro-economic instability were reported as more significant problems than the unavailability of skilled labor. Only 4 percent of

---

8. Using earnings of wage and salary earners in the principal employment only and index of inflation published by INSTAT.

9. For specification of models using both the household survey data and ICA data, see Lassibille, 2007.

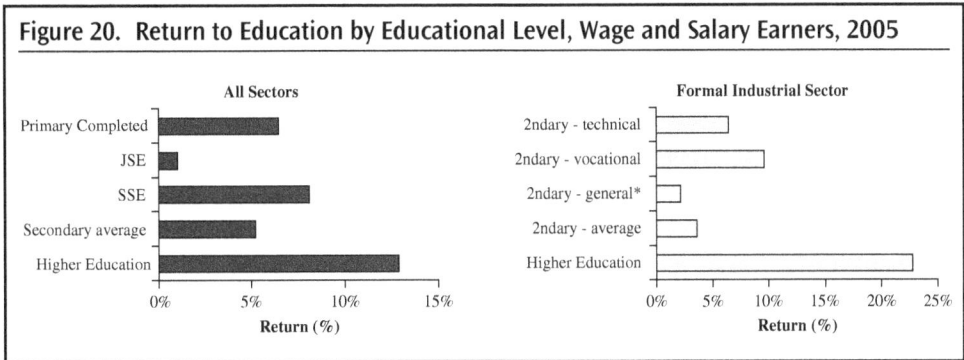

Figure 20. Return to Education by Educational Level, Wage and Salary Earners, 2005

Notes: 1. 'All sectors' figure is calculated from *Enquête Prioritaire auprès des Ménages* 2005 data. It relates only to wage and salary earners. 'Formal industrial sector' figure is calculated from ICA survey data. 2. In the 'all sectors' figure, the rate of return for each level of education is calculated using the coefficients of education estimated in wage regression models and the duration of the cycle. For example, the rate of return to JSE education is calculated by subtracting the coefficient for primary from the coefficient for JSE and dividing by 4 years (the duration of the JSE cycle). 3. In the 'formal industrial sector' figure, the rate of return of the higher education is calculated by comparing all individuals with secondary education. For model specifications and coefficient estimates, see Lassibille, 2007.

employers indicated that this was *the most important* factor. Given the timing of the survey (2005), when the economy was just recovering from a crisis, the small size of the formal manufacturing sector in the country and its concentration in large urban areas, this is not a surprising result. The average time for filling vacancies for skilled labor was estimated to be just two weeks. At current levels of operations, about 23 percent of firms reported a shortage of labor (while 11 percent reported a surplus). Labor shortages were more severe in some sectors such as textiles industry (33 percent), wood (29 percent) and furniture (38 percent) and in medium and small firms (25 percent). The overall shortage of labor was estimated to about 15 percent of the workforce while 35 percent of workers were considered surplus, suggesting that re-allocation of labor across firms and sectors is a major issue.

However, these findings do not indicate that there are no problems related to the availability of skilled labor. Among firms that said that the size of their workforce was sub-optimal, 53 percent said that inability to find skilled labor for the position was the most important reason, far out-ranking other reasons. Moreover, 60 percent of firms also reported that skilled labor availability was a "moderate" to "very severe" obstacle for their future operations.

Large scale surveys often fail to capture critical deficits in key sectors. Madagascar lacks surveys or studies that examine skill needs at the micro level that affect competitiveness and costs in key sectors. The lack of threshold levels of key human capital skills may prevent the emergence of a competitively viable industry. These include skills such as those required to acquire new technology and machinery; design efficient lay out of plants; repair and maintain equipments; use quality control mechanisms and use industrial engineering. Further, surveys, by definition capture only the perceptions of existing firms. They cannot capture whether the constraint prevented new firms from being created.

In the textile and garment industry, the non-availability of middle managers and skilled technicians is cited in two recent studies. Such shortages can erode Madagascar's main competitive advantage (low wages of unskilled workers) by lowering technical productivity and raising the unit cost of labor. Further, with many countries competing in the global market, low costs are no longer the sole competitive advantage (Salinger 2003): "Companies that outperform their competitors in the clothing business are those that have adopted new information systems and management practices... What drives competitiveness in the clothing market today is the ability to bring products to market... just in time." The main requirement is not to increase the overall availability of graduates, but the right type of graduates with the competencies required by enterprises (Box 1).

Box 1. Observations on the Availability of Middle Managers and Skilled Technicians

"The most critical skills shortage is for middle management and frontline personnel where the current employees are mainly expatriates. There appears to be a large number of "middle-management" positions filled by expatriates. This is due to the shortage of local personnel with the necessary competency.

Having to resort to expatriate middle-management has increased the cost of operations in Madagascar. The middle-management shortages are in the technical, administration and management areas. Insofar as industry-specific middle management skills are concerned, these include chemists/colorists and technicians in textile technology and apparel technology. The other middle management skills required to support this industry can be generic in nature and these include production planning, manufacturing operations, mechanical/electrical engineering, administration and management, and entrepreneurship."

Source: Shah and Baru, 2005.

"Most firms use expatriate managers, quality control experts, supervisors, and technicians.... Eventually, a shortage of skilled workers will drive up wage costs and limit the industry's ability to move up the value chain. Madagascar needs to expand its supply of mid-level managers in technical and business areas, e.g. fiber and textiles engineering, technical support personnel, skilled assembly operators, textile arts and fashion design, international branding, market analysts, international sales and contracting, and logistics managers.

In the longer run, Madagascar's cotton-textiles-clothing value-chain will need the support of a more fully developed cluster to succeed. Madagascar lacks the presence of equipment designers and manufacturers, spare parts providers, repair companies, trims manufacturers, training institutes, technical and market research firms, industry-specific marketing and advertising firms, and stronger linkages to end-consumers and clients....

Madagascar needs to expand its supply of mid-level managers in technical and business areas, e.g. fiber and textiles engineering, technical support personnel, skilled assembly operators, textile arts and fashion, international branding, market analysts, international sales and contracting and logistics managers."

Source: Salinger, 2003.

Implications for Post-Basic Education

Despite the apparent lack of aggregate shortage of skilled labor in the short or medium-term, Madagascar needs to re-orient its post-basic education system for several reasons. The first reason is strategic. In order to compete with other countries, even in labor-intensive manufacturing industries but also to develop agriculture, Madagascar needs to raise the stock of human capital. As the analysis of investment by generations shows, decisions taken regarding education take two or three decades to have a perceptible impact on the stock of human capital. Madagascar needs a long-term and consistent policy to expand coverage of primary and junior secondary education at a rapid pace, as well as to gradually expand coverage of post-basic education.

The second reason is that even in the medium-term, Madagascar has to address two problems: (i) the regional availability of skills, to complement its regional development program and (ii) ensuring the type of skills required by the labor market in key growth sectors. The responsiveness of the education system to these challenges will partly determine the ability of Madagascar to compete in a global economy where technology and skills are constantly being upgraded.

CHAPTER 4

Skills for the Labor Market

Improving Relevance and Quality in Post-basic Education and Training

Madagascar's post-basic education system will have to adapt to the new demands of the labor market and the changes induced by the reform of basic education. The aims of education and training at this level are two-fold: (i) meeting the skilled labor requirements of key growth sectors of the economy in the short and medium term, and (ii) preparing for future changes by ensuring that students have a sound foundation of knowledge, skills and attitudes.

A feature of globalization is that the changes in technology and work organization are quickly transmitted across the world. The idea of a single life-time job or even occupation for each worker will soon become a thing of the past, even in Madagascar. Moreover, the rate of obsolescence of skills is more rapid now, with the growth of knowledge and its applications to production. The post-basic education system must not only equip students with current knowledge, but also with the tools to continue their learning. This includes language skills, specific subjects such as mathematics and science, use of information and communication technologies (ICT) as well as learning to learn, reason and apply knowledge.

Countries are often faced with the difficult choice between expanding the supply of education and investing in quality. For Madagascar, this is not really a trade-off. Improving relevance and quality is an imperative. If investments in quality also lead to reduction in repetition and failure rates, they will also increase the supply of places by allowing more students to graduate.

This chapter begins with an analysis of the main growth sectors identified in the MAP, the likely skills requirements of these sectors and the ability of the education and training system to meet these needs. This is followed by a presentation of the features of newly emerging technological occupations and generic skills that are increasingly demanded in the labor market. The chapter then reviews the current status relating to structure, curriculum, teachers and learning materials in each of the sub-sectors—general senior secondary education, TVET and higher education—and priority areas of reform.

Skill Needs in the Growth Sectors of the MAP

The main sectors identified by the MAP may face critical skill shortages. There are few courses in education and training institutions for these new sectors (Table 2). This is due to a lack of a mechanism for employers to express demand for skills to education and training institutions and, in the case of universities, the rigidity in introducing new courses. There is only one mining technical school, despite this being a high priority sector which has attracted considerable foreign direct investment in recent years. Agriculture and tourism, both priority sectors with the potential of absorbing labor, enroll less than 500 students in TVET courses. The textile and garment industry is the largest employer in the formal sector, accounting for a major share of exports. However, there are no courses at the secondary level and a diploma course in textile engineering was introduced only recently as part of the World Bank's Growth Poles project.

Skills constraints can cause wages to rise and erode the competitive advantage of low labor costs. In a skill-intensive sector such as IT, the lack of undergraduates with basic training can prevent the sector from growing. Foreign firms meet these skills needs partly be importing expatriate skilled staff and managers or by sending employees abroad for training.

Technological Occupations in the Knowledge Economy and Science and Technology Education in Madagascar

Technological occupations will become more widespread as Madagascar's economy start integrating technology into production and management across a broad spectrum of economic activity. Such occupations are no longer confined to manufacturing, mining or infrastructure industries; they are found in many sectors, including agriculture and food, tourism, financial services, transportation and supply chains, education and health. Figure 21 illustrates a simple typology of occupations positioned on two education-related dimensions: the theoretical knowledge and analytical skills dimension and the technological skills and competencies dimension.

In the initial phases of transformation of the economy, the vocational and middle level occupations will require greater numbers of trained specialists. However, building up the core of professionals and scientists is necessary in order to create the capacity for technology absorption and application to the local economy.

Applied Science, Engineering and Technology (ASET) courses play an important role in preparing the workforce for these emerging occupations. Madagascar's ASET system is weak, even at the vocational and middle level, but also at the tertiary level. It is further analyzed later in the chapter.

Table 2. Growth Sector Skill Needs and Labor Supply

MAP Sector	Labor	Managerial	Technical	Labor Supply
1. High growth industries				
1.1 Textiles and Garments	♦ Production worker ♦ Technician ♦ Mechanic ♦ Pattern maker	♦ Production floor supervisor ♦ Production planner	♦ Textile engineer	♦ No TVET training courses ♦ Diploma in Textile Engineering: 44 students, 2007
1.2 ICT	♦ Computer support technician ♦ Data entry operator	♦ Project/program manager ♦ Computer/information systems manager	♦ System analyst ♦ Programmer ♦ Computer/information scientist ♦ Software engineer	♦ 178 students enrolled in the *Ecole Nationale d'Informatique*[1]
1.3 Tourism	♦ Food prep worker ♦ Waiter ♦ Housekeeper ♦ Customer service	♦ Food service manager ♦ First-line supervisor	♦ NA	♦ INTH, ISCAM[2] offer vocational 2 yr degree courses ♦ Few graduates ♦ CFPs enroll ~200 students
1.4 Mining	♦ Maintenance personnel ♦ Equipment operator	♦ Mine manager	♦ Geologist ♦ Hydrologist ♦ Engineer	♦ 1 mining technical school
2. Infrastructure				
2.1 Transport (Roads)	♦ Manual laborer ♦ Equipment operator ♦ Surveyor	♦ Manager ♦ Site or first-line supervisor	♦ Civil engineer	♦ Skilled trades: 5000 enrolled in LTPs, 2000 enrolled in CFPs
2.2 Construction	♦ Manual laborer ♦ Carpenter ♦ Ironworker ♦ Mason ♦ Equip. operator ♦ Electrician ♦ Plumber	♦ Manager ♦ Site or first-line supervisor	♦ Civil engineer	♦ Civil engineering programs offered at most vocational or technical schools, ISTs and universities
3. Agriculture	♦ Largely self-employed small scale producers			♦ Technical and vocational: 500 enrolled ♦ Tertiary level: ~1350 enrolled

Source: World Bank analysis of Johanson, 2006; Zaafrane, 2008; and MEN data. *Notes:* 1. *Ecoles Nationales*: highly selective institutions that train engineers and applied scientists. 2. INTH: *Institut National de Tourisme et d'Hôtellerie*. INSCAM—*L'Institut Supérieure de la Communication, des Affaires et du Management*

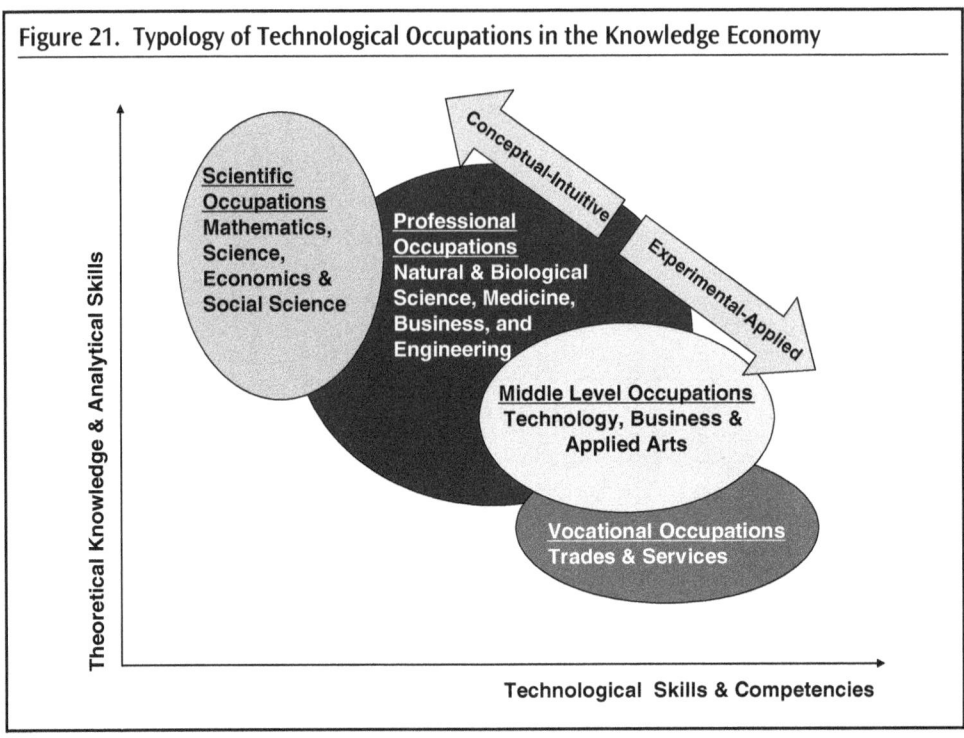

Figure 21. Typology of Technological Occupations in the Knowledge Economy

Source: Mikhail, 2007.

Priorities for Curricular Reform: Focusing on Employability Skills

Employers consider that employability skills are as important as job-specific or technical skills. These skills cannot be taught as a separate subject. They are increasingly embedded across the curriculum and teaching-learning processes. These generic skills are often classified into eight broad areas[10]:

- *Taking initiative*—identifying opportunities not obvious to others; translating ideas into action; generating a range of options; being resourceful; initiating solutions.
- *Communication*—understanding what others are trying to communicate; speaking clearly and directly; writing to the audience's needs; persuading effectively; speaking and writing in more than one language.
- *Teamwork*—working as an individual and as a member of a team; working with people of different backgrounds; defining a role as part of a team; identifying strengths of team members; coaching, mentoring, and giving feedback.

---

10. This illustrative list of "employability skills" was developed by the Department of Education, Science and Training (DEST), the Australian Chamber of Commerce and Industry (ACCI) and the Business Council of Australia (BCA). Source: http://www.dest.gov.au/archive/ty/publications/employability%5Fskills/

- *Technology*—having a range of basic IT skills; applying IT as a management tool; being willing to learn new IT skills; having the health and safety knowledge to use technology.
- *Problem solving*—developing creative, innovative or practical solutions; applying a range of strategies to problem solving; applying problem-solving strategies across a range of areas.
- *Self-management*—having a personal vision and goals; evaluating own performance; articulating own ideas and vision; taking responsibility.
- *Planning*—managing time and priorities; establishing clear project goals and deliverables; allocating people and resources to tasks; planning the use of resources including time; collecting, analyzing, and organizing information to use in continuous improvement and planning.
- *Learning*—managing own learning; contributing to the workplace learning community; using a range of mediums to learn—mentoring, peer support, networking, IT, courses; applying learning to technical issues and people issues.

General employability skills should be central to the reform of curriculum, teaching practices and learning materials at the SSE, TVET and higher education levels. Madagascar's existing system is highly academic, in the case of SSE and higher education, or narrowly specialized and trade/occupation oriented, in the case of TVET. In terms of subjects, the reform should concentrate on the teaching of languages, mathematics, sciences, economics/business and use of IT.

Senior Secondary Education

Structure and Curriculum

At the SSE level, students may choose between general or technical streams, which are provided in separate schools. At the end of the three year cycle (existing duration), students can acquire the baccalauréat by examination, required for entry into tertiary education. The general stream leads to the baccalauréat général (general baccalaureate); the technical stream leads to the baccalauréat technologique (technological baccalaureate) or the baccalauréat technique (technical baccalaureate). Although modeled on the French system, the award does not enable automatic entry to university education.[11] Additional selection mechanisms (review of applications and/or entrance examinations) are applied.

Students in the first year of SSE follow a common curriculum (Figure 22). For the final two years, they choose among three streams: (i) the "*Série A*" for Arts (54 percent of SSE students), (ii) the "*Série C*" for Mathematics, Physics and Chemistry (14 percent of SSE students), and (iii) the "*Série D*" for Life Sciences (32 percent of SSE students). This grouping has not been revised since the 1970s (World Bank 2008). As an example, there is no series for economics and social sciences, despite the growing importance of these disci-

---

11. The French *baccalauréat* is legally a qualifying degree for entry into university.

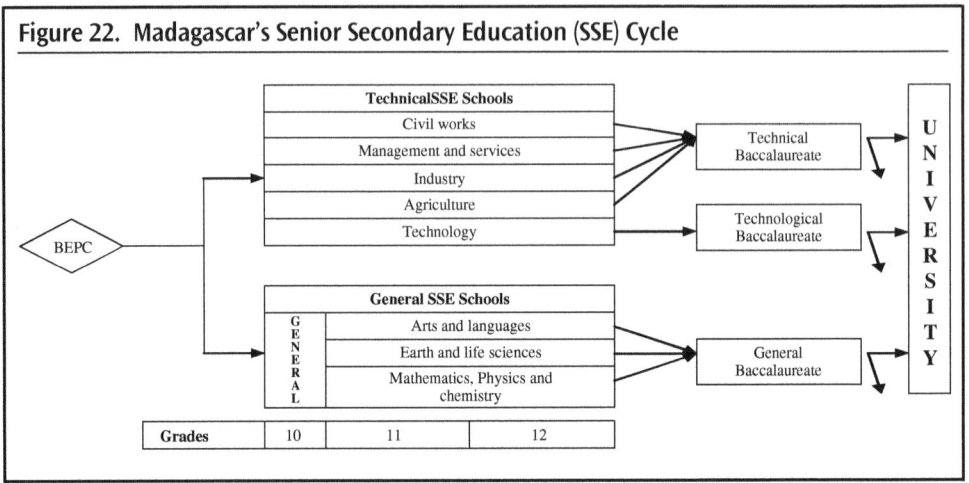

Figure 22. Madagascar's Senior Secondary Education (SSE) Cycle

Source: World Bank 2008.

plines for the economy.[12] The technological and technical streams present a similarly outdated structure, with five streams that are not related to technological occupations. Again, as an example, there are no specific technological/technical *baccalauréat* in hotels or tourism or mining.[13]

Another issue in the curriculum structure is overall class time and core and optional subjects. Madagascar's SSE curriculum is overloaded with students expected to spend up to 1400 hours in class (the range is from 1116–1404 depending on specialization). Students have to take 10–15 subjects. The trend in most countries at the SSE level, as at the JSE level, is to reduce class time in order to allow more time for student self-directed learning and individual support. In most European countries, the annual hours of class instruction varies between 800 to 1000 hours. There are usually about 10 subjects, with a compulsory core of about 6 subjects and an additional four elective subjects.

The over-specialization of the curriculum also has implications for teacher utilization. In contrast to the high student time in classrooms, teachers are expected to teach only 720 hours in class—the average in a sample of 24 countries, including low, middle and high income countries reviewed by OECD/UNESCO was about 910 hours (World Bank 2008). This is partly due to the fragmentation of courses and the requirement for many specialist teachers.

---

12. Madagascar's curriculum follows the old French curriculum. In France, the curriculum has been revised continuously. There are three types of general *Baccalauréat*: *BAC L* (literary—main subjects are French, philosophy and modern languages), *BAC ES* (economic and social sciences), and *BAC S* (scientific—main subjects are mathematics, physics and natural sciences).

13. Again, in France there are four types of technological *Baccalauréat* : *BAC STT* (tertiary sciences and technology), *BAC STI* (industrial sciences and technology), *BAC STL* (laboratory sciences and technology), *BAC SMS* (medical and social sciences); and additional three specific technological *Baccalauréats* for the hotel trade, applied arts, and the techniques of music and dance.

The design of the SSE curriculum is to prepare students for higher education. In fact, however, less than half the students pass the *baccalauréat* and only half of those who pass gain entry to universities. Hence, less than a quarter of those who are in the final year of SSE will go on to university. The curriculum overload, outdated teaching methods and perceived irrelevance of subjects is a factor driving dropout within the cycle. The internal efficiency of the system is closely linked with fundamental problems related to the duration and structure of SSE.

As in the case of the French *baccalauréat,* the content of the terminal examinations places high demands on writing, as most answers are given in essay form (except for mathematics and science, even though some of the latter may also required long answers). The examination does not include individual research or project work done during the course of the year.

An important issue in the context of Madagascar is that the majority of students who fail to pass the examination do not have a qualification that values the 12 years of education they received. The student who has failed the "*Bac*" is little better than a person who holds a JSE certificate in the labor market. The additional three (or two in the new cycle) effectively represents a waste of resources both for the individual and the system.

Teachers

SSE teachers are recruited either with a general university degree (varying from two to four years of duration) or with specialized teacher training at the *Ecoles Normales Supérieures* (ENS), university level institutions, where courses last five years (the period of practice teaching is in addition to this). Only one-third of SSE teachers have a professional teacher training certificate; the majority have some university level education with no teacher training. The duration of training in the ENS is too long and costly for expanding SSE in a cost-effective manner. Further, the rapid evolution of knowledge and need to upgrade curriculum means that much of the knowledge acquired in pre-service training will be obsolete in a few years time. In-service teacher training is very limited, especially in public schools.

Learning Materials

Madagascar's SSE schools lack almost all learning materials, including textbooks. The last World Bank education project (which ended in 2005) provided mathematics textbooks in the last grade of JSE and a minimal library of reference books for each public JSE school and SSE school. There are neither textbooks nor teacher guides; teachers and students rely on teaching notes. The situation is in stark contrast to primary education, where donors have financed books and learning materials on a large scale.

Priorities for Reform

While an overhaul of the curriculum structure is desirable, it poses numerous challenges in a country with limited technical capacity. International experience also shows that system-wide reforms at the higher levels of education are difficult to implement. Conceptually, the reform could be organized around two main pillars:

- *Pillar 1:* An incremental school-based approach to improving quality and efficiency of the academic secondary education, articulated with the reforms in TVET and higher education (see below).
- *Pillar 2:* Introducing new types of secondary technical and vocational schools that are more closely aligned with labor market needs in the priority sectors of the MAP (see section on TVET).

The first pillar would introduce changes in the curriculum, teaching practices and learning materials with technical capacity being built in the Ministry and implementation through voluntary participation of existing public and private schools in a quality improvement program. The latter could be supported through a school development fund. Changes in the curriculum structure would focus on reducing the subject overload and re-organizing the *baccalauréat* series and upgrading the content of curriculum to include general employability and skills, focusing on key subjects. To begin with, improvements in language, mathematics and science and technology, including incorporation of ICT, would be essential. Curriculum upgrading would be supported with provision of new teaching-learning materials and school-based in-service teacher development courses in the schools participating in the program. Over the medium-term, new shorter duration pre-service teacher training programs could be developed in tertiary education institutions. Student assessment in grade 12 could also help to certify competencies acquired, independently of the terminal examination. The development of a qualifications framework (discussed later in this report) will also help in ensuring the acceptability of such certification.

The second pillar would introduce diversity in the types of secondary schools and also enable greater access in rural areas. Three models are under consideration by the Ministry: "magnet," career, and comprehensive schools (Box 2).

The design of both pillars of the reform should include a strong component to address equity (both income and geographic). This could be done by building it into the school development fund, targeted scholarship programs and criteria for building new schools.

TVET

Structure and Curriculum

Broadly speaking, TVET covers education and training from grade 6 to the tertiary level. However, in Madagascar, there is little articulation between the secondary level and tertiary level in TVET. Formerly, this was partly due to the fact that there were separate Ministries for school education, TVET and higher education, but even with a single Ministry the structure is fragmented (Figure 23). In addition, other Ministries (Labor, Agriculture, Public Works) run public institutions or authorize private training centers for their sectors.

> **Box 2. Alternative Models for Secondary Education**
>
> **Magnet Schools**
> - Usually urban
> - High quality specialized preparation for university
> - Science and Technology MS, Mathematics MS, Foreign language MS
> - Elite—draw best students from the system through "examination" and competitive application
> - Highly qualified faculty—the best teach the best
> - University partnerships
> - High cost
> - Public and/or private finance
>
> **Career Secondary Schools**
> - Focus on one career path (tourism, textiles, health sciences, computers)
> - Located near employers
> - Motivated students with good general knowledge
> - Core academic curriculum-examined subjects
> - Professional curriculum, taught by professionals
> - More student time—in a week, more months or years
> - School/work collaboration through internships
> - Cost depends on the skills demanded in the career
> - Substantial industry financial support
>
> **Comprehensive Schools**
> - Often rural
> - Several curriculum
>   - Academic for higher education
>   - General education: less demanding, for post-secondary education
>   - Vocational courses for local employment
> - Accept all students in area with complete JSE
> - Students can choose from all curriculum but have to meet graduation requirements—20–30 percent electives
> - Strong student guidance counseling
> - Vocational curriculum can be more costly than academic or general
>
> *Source:* Middleton, 2007.

TVET should provide trained personnel for the labor market but Madagascar's system, despite some positive changes over the last five years, is still not effective in this respect. The system is characterized by a highly formal structure, with seven types of formal qualifications with relatively long courses, two to three years each, with only one entry point and one exit point. There are two main types of TVET: CFP (vocational training centers

Figure 23. Structure of Madagascar TVET system, 2007 (Pre-reform)

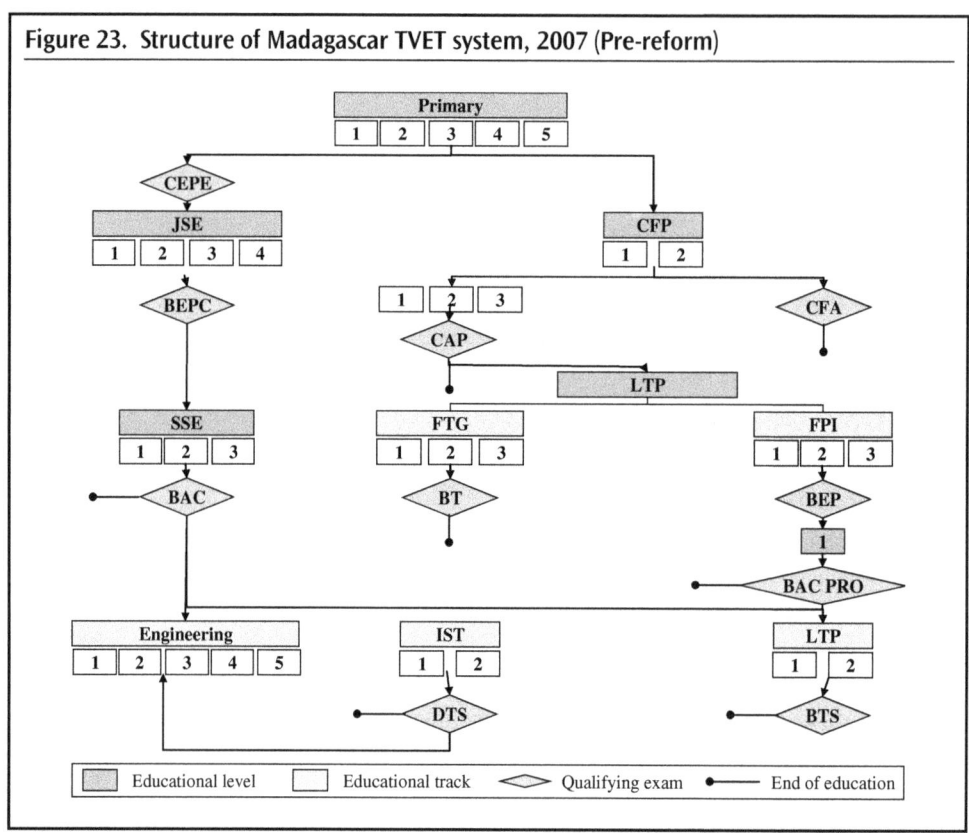

Institutions	Programs	Qualifications
CFP—Centre de Formation Professionnelle	FPI—Formation Professionnel Initial	CFA—Certificat de Foin d'Apprentissage
LTP—Lycée Technique et Professionnel	FTG—Formation Professionnel General	CAP—Certificat d'Aptitude Professionnelle
IST—Institut Supérieur Technologique	FPQ—Formation Professionnel Qualificant	BEP—Brevet d'Etude Professionnelle
		Bac Pro—Baccalauréat Professionnel
		Bac T—Baccalauréat Technologique

Notes: 1. The *Institut Supérieur Technologique* offers three qualifications—DTS (Bacc + 2 years), *Diplôme de Technicien Supérieur Spécialisé* (DTSS) (Bacc + 3 years), and *Diplôme d'Ingénieur de l'IST* (DIIST) (Bacc + 4.) 2. Short-duration training without a formally recognized certificate—offered in both CFPs and LTPs—is not shown in the diagram.

operating at junior secondary level) and LTP (technical/vocational schools at the senior secondary level). Enrollment in public CFPs is limited, amounting to only 6 percent of junior secondary enrollments. Enrollment in public LTPs accounts for about 10 percent of enrollment at the SSE level.

Most training institutions at LTP level train for a particular sector (industrial, commercial or agriculture) while CFPs enrollments are concentrated in just two broad fields—civil works and industry. There are major gaps in TVET provision. As noted earlier, enrollment is limited in the areas important for the priority sectors of the MAP. Training for agricultural occupations and the informal sector hardly exists.

LTPs and CFPs teach only a limited range of technical skills for narrowly defined occupation. Students specialize in specific trades; for example, those enrolled in building trades concentrate on one trade such as masonry, rather than the range of skills involved in simple construction—masonry, framing, roofing, plumbing and electricity. A broad knowledge of the industry, general employability skills or workplace competencies for the industry are not built into the curriculum.

Although the programs teach only a narrow range of skills, curriculum and examinations are overloaded in terms of the number of subjects, leading to limited mastery of core competencies. The courses tend to be fragmented with students in the various LTP programs taking 12–14 different classes per week. In some cases, students take courses in three languages (Malagasy, French, English); the limited exposure of two or three hours per week each is insufficient to attain fluency in communication.

A few important innovations have been introduced. Public training institutions are now allowed to provide training according to local needs. Training for in-service employees can be short-term and variable in length and a diploma for technicians has been introduced.

Teaching methods are outdated, emphasizing lecture and note-taking by students, rather than discussion, problem solving and group work. Examinations and assessment are based on theoretical knowledge and employers do not participate in the process.

Teachers/Instructors

Between 1998 and 2005, the number of teachers in public CFPs and LTPs remained constant at about 1000, due to a hiring freeze in force for public sector employees. As a result, most of the teaching staff are between 55 to 58 years old, close to the retirement age of 60 years. Departures due to retirement will cause a drop in teacher availability. Although most of the staff are qualified, especially in the LTPs, about 20 percent had qualifications at the level at which they taught and only 9 percent had engineering degrees. One difficulty in adapting courses to labor market needs is the lack of teachers in the required field and the inability to adjust teacher positions as they belong to the civil service. Prior practical experience in industry is not required and most do not have any knowledge of industry operations.

There is no pre-service training for TVET instructors and in-service training is limited. The main in-service training institution is the National Institution for Training (INFOR), which reported training 250 instructors in 2005. However, there are no transparent mechanisms for selecting instructors for training and due to limited industry exchanges, instructors cannot remain up to date with technological improvements.

Learning Materials

These are almost universally lacking and students must copy or study teacher notes from the blackboard.

In countries with strong systems of TVET, external parties participate in the examinations to ensure objectivity. The examination load on students is heavy, with students in LTPs taking examinations in 9–11 different subjects (compared with six for students in general *lycées.*)

Priorities for Reform

The reform of primary and junior basic education is a positive development for TVET and provides the opportunity to introduce flexibility and relevance of programs. Entrants into TVET will have more education (at least seven years of primary education), and this will allow the general education content to be eliminated from these courses. A major question, however, is whether to provide vocational training after 7 years of primary or after 10 years of basic education. International experience suggests that it is better to defer specialization until students are able to choose their occupations. Employers do not often require long-duration training for entry level workers, preferring to train them on the job. Madagascar's policy is to move towards provision of basic education for all children. The policy for junior secondary education also includes the provision of open schools, which could integrate a high level of vocational content. Looking to the future, therefore, it seems more appropriate to start vocational training after 10 years of basic education.

If vocational training is provided after seven years of primary, it should be possible to cut the length of most vocational training in CFPs to *six-nine months*—compared to *two–three years* at present. This would double or triple the number of graduates. In any case, CFPs should not provide a three year program of studies in parallel with lower secondary education.

Technician training at the senior secondary level (LTPs) should be expanded and a more balanced regional distribution should be achieved through the involvement of the regions and communes.

Introduction of new courses for the priority sectors should be the focus of reform of curriculum, teaching and assessment methods. Concentration on fewer subjects, with more emphasis on science and mathematics, would be advisable for quality improvement. Reducing the duration of courses to the time required for teaching the skills, polyvalent training, focus on generic skills and a modular approach to facilitate easy entry and exit would be highly desirable.

A major challenge is to train teachers and provide in-service training. Due to limited resources, the focus should be on the new courses. Designing a system of financing in-service training and enabling INFOR to become self-financing would be necessary. Teacher development reforms are discussed more extensively at the end of the chapter.

The most important challenge in improving quality and relevance, however, is to involve employers in defining training needs and in examining and certifying skills acquisition. This is dealt with in greater detail in chapter 8 on governance mechanisms.

Tertiary Education

Madagascar's tertiary education system consists of six universities, two non-university institutes offering 2-year technological courses, one distance education organization in the public sector, and about 20 non-university institutes in the private sector. The public universities absorb four-fifths of students and close to 60 percent of them are in the University of Antananarivo and another 14 percent in the University of Toamasina. The remaining four universities have between 1,500–4,000 students, far less than the minimum enrollment size for a multi-disciplinary university offering undergraduate and postgraduate courses. Enrollment in distance education, which operates through 24 regional centers, has been declining continuously for the last 10 years, and is currently at 15 percent of total tertiary enrollment while enrollment in the private sector has risen to about 8 percent (starting from 0) in the same period.

Structure and Curriculum

Most university programs are still based on a traditional educational model for long courses, which existed before in most continental European countries and comprised three cycles of varying lengths. The hierarchy of awards is based on the number of years after the *baccalauréat*. The first cycle of two years leads to the *Diplôme d'Enseignement Universitaire Général* (DEUG—General University Diploma, or Bac+2); the second cycle leads to the *licence or maîtrise*, of two-three years duration (Bac+3/4); and the third cycle leads to a higher level professional degree (*Diplôme d'Etudes Supérieures Spécialisées—DESS—* in one year) or a doctoral degree.

This structure has been replaced in France and in most European countries, which have re-organized university programs to bachelor's-master's-doctoral degrees (*Licence—Maîtrise—Doctorat* or LMD), in line with international trends. The bachelor's degrees are of three years duration and master's of two years duration.

In Madagascar, the first degree still requires five years of study in many disciplines. The first two years leading to DEUG emphasize basic theoretical training in mathematics or sciences and are not considered adequate for jobs suitable for undergraduates. The most common award for engineering, for example, is the *Diplôme D'Ingénieur* which is at the level of BAC+5. The LMD reform has just begun, with the publication of the framework earlier in 2008; regulations to guide reform are close to publication.

The Malagasy university curriculum structure contributes to the poor internal efficiency noted earlier, with high rates of failure, dropout and repetition. For example, in applied science, engineering and technology courses, Madagascar produces a meager number of undergraduates and engineers, despite an enrollment of over 9000 students (about 20 percent of the total enrollment). In 2005/06, the public institutions produced 508 graduates at the diploma level, and another 334 graduates from the 2 year post-secondary technical program, offered in the two ISTs (total of over 842). While most of the IST graduates have awards that lead to employment, most of the former continue with further studies as their diploma is not valued in the job market. There were 583 graduates with Bac+3 and 426 with Bac+4. The number of engineering graduates was only 294 (Figure 24).

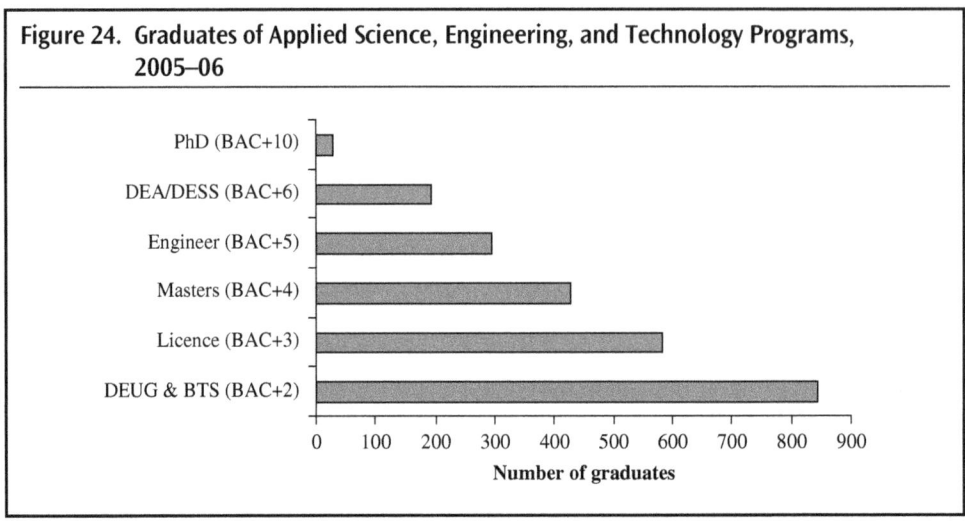

Source: World Bank analysis of MEN data.

The ISTs, which have short-duration courses that train higher level technicians, however, enroll less than 1000 students in total, about 11 percent of enrollment in ASET programs and only 2 percent of tertiary enrollment.

Curriculum overload is evident at the tertiary level as well. In ASET programs, students normally attend 40 hours per week of formal lectures and lab work; this is well over the average of 26–30 hours observed in most of the world. Although 16 hours are supposed to be for experimental/practical work, there is little of this due to the dilapidated conditions of laboratories and workshops and materials. The most common method of teaching is lecture, with no written materials. Students have no time for project work, personal study or library work. The legal obligation for university teachers is only 5 hours a week, an unusually low work load, the rationale for which is the need for them to devote 15–20 hours to research. In practice, there is no research work done, and faculty members either teach supplementary hours, paid for by universities, and/or in private institutions. Supplementary teaching is a means to add to teacher earnings, and now exceeds official teaching hours by a large margin. This discussed further in the chapter on costs and financing. Apart from the high costs this generates, the practice also has perverse effects on teaching quality with little time left for preparation and evaluation.

Faculty

The average age of teaching staff in universities is 55. Again, as in TVET, institutions a hiring freeze on civil servants, in force for almost two decades (except for priority sectors such as primary education and health) has created this crisis situation, which threatens the very foundation of the university system. There are no venues for faculty development. Many teachers try, on their own initiative, to secure research projects in collaboration with foreign universities.

Learning Resources

The quality of libraries and laboratories is poor, where they exist at all. Most of the five regional universities have virtually nothing. Libraries have not had major acquisitions for more than ten years, ICT infrastructure is either very poor or non-existent, and access to the internet is slow and unreliable. For applied science and technology courses, the conditions are degraded—there is little or no equipment or supplies in laboratories and workshops. In most cases, there are no qualified laboratory technicians to repair the equipment or support the practical experiential component of the program. Buildings are dilapidated; the University of Toliara runs the majority of its courses in temporary structures built for construction workers three decades ago. There are some exceptions to this rule, including ISTs and some quasi-independent bodies within universities. Examples of these include *IHSM, ENS, Laboratoire de Biochimie Fondamentale et Appliquée.* These organizations are distinguished by their ability to raise resources, utilize them for improving learning, and manage their facilities.

Priorities for Reform

The extremely degraded state of universities, the cumulative effect of years of neglect, means that the needs are enormous. Careful prioritization is required, primarily because resources will be limited in the medium term. The first priority is to select courses and disciplines, at the undergraduate level, that are important for the economic development of the country. Courses in applied sciences, engineering and technology, teacher training, health, communications, economics and management/business studies would be appropriate choices. The second is to expand the provision of the short-duration courses for training of higher level technicians, possibly through the creation of new ISTs in different regions, or by enabling universities to offer similar courses with new arrangements for quality control, employer participation and governance.

The third priority reform to improve relevance and quality is to accelerate the introduction of the move towards the LMD in a structured manner, targeting specific priority courses at the undergraduate level. This reform, supported by adequate funding for course development, faculty development and additional infrastructure, ICT and materials, would enable revision of curriculum and teaching methods, including introduction of generic employability skills across courses. It would also vastly improve student flow and internal efficiency. A variety of methods have been tried in European countries, including in the EU accession countries, some of which may be more relevant to Madagascar (Box 3).

In addition to the LMD reform, faculty development in critical areas can be organized through multi-day seminars and workshops. These could focus on general capacity building topics such as research methods, ICT utilization for instruction and research, teaching methods and improvement, and presentations of overviews of state-of-the-art research and literature in specific priority fields. Further, a program of staff development can be established to encourage students to obtain master's and PhDs in required disciplines, to fill the requirement of teachers. These would have to be complemented with changes in faculty recruitment and remuneration, which are discussed further in this report.

Box 3. Strategies for Shifting to LMD in Selected European Countries

Norway

- In 2003, the Bachelor-Master structure was introduced by law with a specification of general guidelines for the design of new study programs and degrees.
- There is a transition phase until 2005, and thereafter all study programs have to be converted.
- At the universities the boards are often involved in decision-making about the new study programs.

Netherlands

- In 2002, the new higher education law established that the "hogescholen" (colleges and their equivalents) as of 2002/03 had to convert their old study programs to correspond with the new Bachelor-Master structures within two years.
- Newly developed study programs had to follow the Bachelor-Master structure, while the conversion of existing study programs is regulated into the new structure until 2007 as a discretionary clause.
- The number of Bachelor and Master study programs greatly increased since the introduction of the higher education law of 2002.

Austria

- With the university law of 2002, Austrian universities became legally independent and are now able to decide themselves about the conversion of existing study programs into the graded structure.
- Some subjects have already completely converted to the Bachelor-Master model (especially in IT and the technical disciplines), while the conversion in law, theology and the humanities and cultural disciplines especially is slow.

France

- Based on several ministerial decrees of spring 2002, the implementation process of Bachelor and Master study programs took place in chronologically consecutive regional waves:
  - 1st wave 2003 wave to 2006 at 23 universities;
  - 2nd wave 2004 to 2007 at 32 universities;
  - 3rd wave 2005 to 2008 at 16 universities;
  - 4th wave 2006 to 2009 at 17 universities.
- The length of the waves corresponds to the four-year contract regional universities have with the Ministry of Education, which is the basis for negotiating the budget.
- All new study programs will first be developed at faculty level and then have to be passed by the Administration Council and the Higher Education Council of each institution before being submitted to the Ministry for approval.

Hungary

- A decree was issued in 2004 for the conversion process to be followed by a higher education law at the beginning of 2005.
- Within the framework of national working groups, "education and competences requirements" are defined, on the basis of which concrete study programs can be developed.
- From 2006/2007 comprehensive Bachelor study programs are to be set up at all Hungarian universities. The Master study programs are similarly to be developed at a later stage.

(continued)

> **Box 3. Strategies for Shifting to LMD in Selected European Countries** (*Continued*)
>
> **Albania**
> - By way of sub-legal acts, the organization of the first cycle studies in some pilot branches/courses of study has been finalized in accordance with the "Bologna Declaration".
> - With the signing of the "Bologna Declaration" in September 2003, its application has been effective in certain pilot courses of study during the academic year 2004–2005 in 6 higher schools.
> - Working teams have been set up in order to oversee the system.
>
> *Source:* Alesi and others 2005; and Bologna Process National Report on Albania 2005.

Madagascar could also consider making greater use of partnerships with foreign universities. At the moment, there are a few isolated cases of collaboration, including those that lead to joint degrees. Many developing countries in Asia and Anglophone Africa are systematically using such partnerships to build the capacity of public and private institutions in selected areas and to create models of excellence with new curriculum, teaching and assessment methods, student-centered and resource-based learning, and modern methods of management. Examples of partnerships range from franchising and twinning arrangements, joint degrees and branch campuses fully owned by foreign universities (Bashir, 2007). The range of possible partners is also increasing, with high quality institutions in developing countries competing with universities from the advanced countries. International experience shows that strong government commitment and leadership, as well as sound technical analysis, is required to maximize the benefits from such partnerships and to avoid the risk of "fly-by-night" operators. A clear policy, sound regulatory framework for foreign partners and quality assurance and accreditation measures are essential pre-requisites to reduce risks to both sides.

Finally, as in the other sub-sectors, reforms implemented by institutions have the greatest chance of success. These would require innovative funding mechanisms, such as competitive grants, and changes to the governance structure of universities, which are discussed later in this report.

Teacher Training, An Overarching Reform Priority

Teachers are the essential component of any strategy to improve educational quality. The training and professional development of teachers should be one of the main priorities of the post-basic education reform in Madagascar, cutting across post-basic education subsectors. Because of the specificity of TVET, the feasibility of expanding INFOR to train TVET instructors should be evaluated. This section will focus on SSE teachers and university faculty.

The aging of the teaching force constitutes both a challenge and an opportunity—a challenge because additional numbers will be required soon, and an opportunity because the whole teaching force can be renewed over a period of 15 years, provided appropriate strategies are chosen. The precise number of new teachers required per year will depend on the scale of the expansion of post-basic education, but under all scenarios thousands of teachers will need to be trained over the next ten years. Specific reform priorities for SSE and for tertiary institutions are as follows:

Senior Secondary Teachers

Various strategies will have to be developed, taking into account the availability of institutions and the level of resources. Given limited institutional training capacity, including the low number of current teacher educators, it is best to consider a two-pronged strategy:

- Begin with in-service teacher development programs, which are linked to reforms implemented at the school level. The focus of such programs should be to improve classroom instruction, familiarize teachers with new materials and teaching methods, and support teachers in implementing them. Such methods are not appropriate for deepening knowledge of subject matter. School-based instructional improvement could therefore be complemented by additional courses for enhance subject mastery, delivered during holidays.
- Reform of pre-service education has to address the major question of whether there should be an integrated teacher education degree, or an additional teacher certification after a bachelor's or master's degree. In Madagascar's context, the latter is probably the best option given the need to rapidly increase the supply of secondary school teachers. To get new teachers into classrooms as quickly as possible, the design of teacher certification programs could combine periods of teaching with periods of study.

Universities' capacity to train additional SSE teachers rapidly will remain constrained. Encouraging the growth of private teacher training institutions, with accredited programs, is one way to expand supply. The government could support this development through an appropriate regulatory framework, public subsidies for certain categories of students (in certain disciplines or for certain regions), and support for curriculum and material development. Another promising avenue is the use of open and distance education, which is being extensively used in many African countries. Finally, a serious effort must be made to review the training of teacher educators and to expand their supply.

In developing strategies, it would best to take the proposed expansion of junior secondary education into account, as well as the intended reform of junior secondary curriculum. The MEN proposes to do a detailed study for planning teacher training in junior secondary education, and this could be extended to SSE. The study should do the following: (i) estimate the annualized need for teachers, by subject, particularly for science, math and language; (ii) design teacher competencies for each category of teacher; (iii) develop alternative options for pre-service and in-service teacher education and training, taking into account costs, capacity building requirements, and ability to scale up through the private sector and/or open and distance learning; and (iv) evaluate teacher compensation and career development opportunities.

University Faculty

One of the key challenges in post-basic reform is the need to develop a dynamic faculty corps who will train new teachers and lead research in areas critical to Madagascar's growth economy. Today, many of Madagascar's university professors are nearing retirement age, creating a window of opportunity to restructure the faculty corps to meet those needs.

Recruitment of New Faculty. Although exact numbers will have to be estimated, Madagascar is expected to need several hundred new, high quality professors over the next few years. New faculty should be PhD holders in high priority disciplines, with a long academic life ahead of them. A clear recruitment strategy must be developed, to ensure that newly recruited faculty meets these requirements. Before launching a major effort to recruit, the Ministry should consider the following critical issues:

- Method of allocating positions and priority areas
- Quality expectations
- Additional training for non-PhD holders
- Contract versus regular appointments.

Method of Allocating Positions. In order to re-orient university programs, continuation of the existing method of "automatic allocations" based on unmanaged enrollment growth or university decisions alone should be avoided. Priorities need to be set both by universities and the Ministry taking into account the priority fields of expansion set by the government, based on labor market/economic development needs. The selection of priority fields should be done by the Ministry, which is the major funder and which should steer the universities towards the economic development needs of the country. The Ministry's criteria for selection of priority fields should be based on labor market needs while universities can be invited to participate by identifying a few priority fields with a justification for each. The exact rules for reviewing proposals and allocating positions would need to be developed.

Quality Expectations. The ideal is to insist that all new faculty have PhDs, but this may not be possible in the short run. Those without should be sent immediately for training for the PhD after being hired. Those positions should, however, be conditional on completing the PhD in three years at an approved program. Because domestic research capacity is limited, the possibility of Ph.D. training abroad in low-cost locations should be investigated. Because Madagascar is a member of SADC, South Africa is an attractive option, but opportunities are also available in Asian countries. Bilateral programs with European countries should also be explored. The Ministry's main role would be identify potential approved programs, secure funding and agreements, develop regulations and facilitate the rapid training of young recruits.

Age Restrictions. The majority of people should be under forty years of age with most of them fresh PhDs in their late 20s or early thirties. This would require setting age caps on new recruitment and the methods for doing this should be investigated.

Contract Versus Regular Appointments. The Ministry should consider recruiting all new faculty on some kind of contract employment with renewal and salary increases contingent of demonstrated high quality performance. Contracts could be set for an initial period of three years. In order to attract good faculty, and to reflect the lower level of security and higher performance expectations, the original hiring and first renewal should be based on higher average salary payments. Further renewals could lead to promotion in rank as well as higher than average salary increase. Faculty whose positions were not renewed would not be able to continue after a grace period. Once the broad strategy is adopted, the Ministry needs to prepare detailed regulations and the process must be implemented transparently. However, changes to the method of paying supplementary hours to existing faculty need to be introduced in order to ensure that contract teachers are being rewarded for higher performance and incentives are not skewed.

Faculty Development. A strategy for faculty development needs to be developed, taking into account both immediate short-term needs and longer term faculty development. In order to address short term needs, a series of workshops could be organized by the Ministry or one of the universities, focusing on upgrading content knowledge in critical areas, improving teaching and learning (including use of new materials and the Internet), methods for outcome assessment and research methods to keep up with developments in the fields of specialization. While implementation could be decentralized to the universities, the planning and funding is best undertaken centrally in order to make the best use of resources. Universities could identify lists of potential speakers and presenters, with the Ministry facilitating the process.

Long term faculty development should include the provision of research support. Given the need to concentrate funding on instruction, the amount allocated for research support has to be carefully targeted and monitored. Priority should be given to young scholars supplemented by competitive funding for other research. The focus would be initially on applied research.

CHAPTER 5

Access and Equity in Post-basic Education

Madagascar's urgent priority is to improve the quality and relevance of its post-basic education. However, it also has to put in place strategies to expand post-basic education, for several reasons. First, increasing the enrollment ratio in post-basic education from its current low levels is a strategic imperative for Madagascar. It is required to raise the educational attainment of its workforce over the next 15–20 years and create a threshold of human capital to participate in the knowledge economy. Second, there is a need to ensure greater participation from low income groups, which are currently virtually excluded from senior secondary and tertiary education. Expanding educational opportunities for the poor will have a tremendous impact on raising incomes and social mobility and cohesion. Another aspect of equity in Madagascar's context is the regional dimension, especially as promoting regional and rural development is one of the pillars of the MAP. Third, the government can ill afford to ignore the pressure of increasing numbers generated within the education system, by a combination of demographic growth and higher completion rates in basic education.

Unless measures to increase access are put in place soon, there is a risk that scarce resources will be absorbed by expanding the existing wasteful and inefficient system. The pressure to provide places to thousands of additional students each year cannot be ignored by political authorities. Instead of adopting *ad hoc* measures that can undercut the reforms to improve quality and governance, it is better to use the coming years to diversifying access and enhancing equity.

Policies to improve access and equity can relate to increasing public provision, providing public funding to stimulate demand and offset private costs as well as making greater use of new delivery systems and the private sector. This chapter considers each of these factors in turn.

Forecast Demographic Boom to Increase Demand for Post-basic Education

Between 2005 and 2015, the age cohorts corresponding to post-basic education, 15–24 year olds, will grow by about 3.3 percent per year. The growth rate will slow down to about 2.4 percent per year between 2015 and 2025. Between 2005 and 2025, the number of 15–19 year olds will increase by 60 percent from approximately 2 million to 3.2 million, and the number of 20–24 year olds by 76 percent from 1.7 million to 2.8 million.

Hence, provision must be made to accommodate thousands more students even at current participation rates and in efficiency indicators. An improvement in the latter would lead to automatically raise the number of students who wish to go to higher levels of education. For example, a rise in the pass rate of the *baccalauréat* would increase the number of eligible candidates for higher education. The former may be desirable in itself, yet student flow into universities must be managed without denying them opportunities for further learning.

Increasing Public Provision

Madagascar's main constraint in increasing public provision will be the availability of public resources. Whatever alternatives are found, public provision will continue to be necessary in rural areas in SSE and TVET, and also in tertiary level courses. One way to increase provision with limited resources is to seek ways to reduce unit costs. Measures to reduce the cost of inputs into the educational process (such as construction or equipment) are important but they are not the only way. The cost of provision of a school can be raised because of an over-specialized curriculum, increasing the requirements in teachers and rooms. Further, unit costs (of a graduate) can also be substantially increased due to high levels of dropout, repetition and failure in the system.

Hence, the reforms of structure, curriculum, teaching practices and assessment methods discussed in the previous chapter are necessary not only to enhance relevance and quality. They can contribute significantly to increasing access, by reducing the cost of provision and improving the internal efficiency of the system.

One implication of this is that any new public provision should be integrally linked to phasing in the new curriculum structures and quality improvement measures and to improving internal efficiency. The government could take a decision, for example, to establish new public secondary schools only with new curriculum and pedagogic models. This would also be aligned with the strategy to implement reforms using a school-based model.

Pedagogical choices can greatly influence costs of infrastructure and equipment, which are more important at higher levels of education than in primary education. The cost of a laboratory can increase by a factor of 5 depending on how experiments are conducted. A demonstration experiment by a teacher is the lowest cost option (but may have limited pedagogical value). Adding computerized equipment for a teacher will add to costs, but not significantly. However, providing equipment and space for small groups of students to perform their own experiments greatly raises costs.[14] Decisions to provide integrated or separate laboratories for the sciences will also greatly affect costs.

---

14. Based on informal estimates collected in the context of the World Bank's Secondary Education in Africa regional study. A cost of a chemistry laboratory for 40 students where a teacher does demonstration experiments would be about 10,000 Euros. If students are divided into 13 groups of 3 with each group

Hence, rationalization in the provision of expensive facilities and ensuring their full utilization is an imperative, especially in SSE and TVET. One possibility is to group SSE schools by "series" and provide laboratories only for those studying the science series to benefit from economies of scale. Another is to create such facilities in selected SSE schools and enable a network of schools to access them. Such models are more likely to work in urban areas than in rural areas, where low population density means that new models have to be developed. A variety of models would probably be required, given Madagascar's diversity and size. In all cases, the design and implementation challenges demand careful management, experimentation and evaluation before upscaling.

In the case of tertiary education, universities could be selected to specialize in particular disciplines (especially in science and technology) to ensure economies of scale.

In order to promote regional equity and greater access to under-served populations, where public provision would be necessary (sometimes at higher than average cost, due to low density populations), explicit criteria need to be built into the planning and budgeting cycle. At the moment, there are no established planning and allocation criteria. The Ministry could effectively adapt the model developed for the provision of primary schools which balances the need to provide universal access to grades 1–5 within 2 km of every village with the need to provide more grades 6 and 7 in the new primary cycle. The model involves a two stage allocation process. In the first stage, the Ministry develops a financial envelope for each district, using a weighted formula taking into account the primary school-age population, population density and the enrollment ratio. In the second stage, each district determines allocation by communes/communities taking into account two priorities: providing a school to villages without any facility and ensuring that schools with incomplete cycles are upgraded.

Demand-Side Interventions

Between 1960 and 1972, Madagascar had a scholarship program to help students from poor families attend school. Since then there have been no systematic government programs in school education, although tertiary level students continue to get scholarships. While scholarships were theoretically destined to help the neediest students, in practice they have become an entitlement over the past decade. Today almost all students enrolled in a public tertiary education institution receive a government scholarship. The proportion of beneficiaries rose from 52 percent in 1993 to 83 percent in 2006.

The current situation accentuates inequalities in access to post-basic provision, by giving scholarships to all tertiary level students, almost all of whom come from the richest 20 percent of families in Madagascar, while providing none at lower levels. Designing an effective scholarship program to promote participation of poor students in SSE and TVET should be a high priority. A critical issue of the design is how to determine transparent eligibility criteria. In low-income agricultural countries, determining family income is not easy. One possibility is to target students from rural areas or from specific districts with low

---

provided with equipment, the cost would be 45,000 Euros. Providing additional computerized equipment to teachers and students would raise the cost to 55,000 Euros. Costs of physics and biology labs are estimated to be higher.

enrollment ratios, since poverty in Madagascar is geographically localized. Targeting girls may also be an option; however, one study found that selecting just girls when both boys and girls in poor families cannot access secondary education posed problems for the family. Another important issue is to lower administration and supervision costs.[15]

The university scholarship program meets neither equity nor efficiency criteria. First, students enrolled in private tertiary education institutions are not eligible for government scholarships and there is no student loan system in Madagascar. This creates a discriminatory situation from an equity viewpoint and represents a serious constraint to the expansion of the private tertiary education sector which the Government supposedly wants to encourage. Second, although scholarships are provided to all students, the absolute amounts are low as scarce resources are spread thinly. Moreover, there are significant differences in the way each institution, or sometimes even each school/institute within a university, applies the rule. At the University of Antsiranana, for example, first-year students get a scholarship in the Polytechnic and the Technical Teacher Training School, but only 40 percent of incoming students get a scholarship at the Faculty of Science. Students who repeat the year keep only half of the scholarship, but at the University of Antananarivo they keep the full scholarship. Students enrolled in the new Business Administration Institute are not eligible for scholarships. At the ISTs, students who do not maintain a good attendance record lose their scholarship. Also, the proportion varies significantly from one university to the other, with a relative low of 59 percent at the University of Mahajanga and a high of 90 percent at the University of Toamasina.

There is considerable international experience in the design and implementation of student aid programs at the tertiary level and these lessons should be used in deciding on appropriate options. Both scholarships and loans can be considered, though experience shows that students from the poorest backgrounds cannot rely on loans alone but also require additional funding in the form of grants. Simplifying the administration of loans is crucial, including establishing easily verifiable eligibility criteria and reducing the documentation and collateral required for application. Ensuring a high level of collection is crucial for the long-term sustainability of the scheme.

The Ministry of Education could review the student aid policy along the following lines:

- Assess whether current amounts are sufficient for those students who are entirely dependent on the scholarship as their only source of income, and increase the amounts as needed.
- Define more strict need-related eligibility criteria to ensure proper targeting of the limited financial aid resources.
- Link the prospects for keeping a scholarship on a continuous basis to the academic performance of students.

---

15. "Feasibility Study on Conditional Cash Transfers in Madagascar." World Bank Consultant report. November 2005. The study looked at the US Ambassador's Girls' Scholarship Program, sponsored by the US government in Madagascar. The program has existed for six years and operated in all six Regions. Roughly 1,000 girls benefit from this program and get a bursary of 100 dollars per year (10 dollars each month during the school year). The money is only meant to support the school expenses for the girl concerned and up to 30 percent of the money can be used on food. This rigidity of the program and close supervision entailed considerable costs and time. (World Bank, 2007a).

- Undertake a feasibility study for the establishment of a student loan system.
- Assess the feasibility of replacing scholarships for first-year students with loans that could be forgiven at the end of the year for those students who pass onto second year.
- Evaluate the possibility of granting scholarships to needy, academically qualified students who want to enroll in an accredited private tertiary education institution.

Open and Distance Learning Systems[16]

Open and Distance Learning (ODL) at both the school and tertiary level can greatly expand access by introducing flexibility in learning for those who are unable to continue long duration studies or those who wish to resume studies, as well as by reducing costs of delivery. The latter is achieved through using different settings and through use of part-time teachers as tutors. Madagascar has some experience in using distance learning at the tertiary level (CENTEMAD), which got off to a promising start but now is in a state of decline. Not only have enrollments halved over the last ten years, but the cost of producing a graduate is estimated to be higher than in face-to-face learning due to high dropout and repetition rates. Better designed programs are now being launched in primary education (teacher training through radio) and in junior secondary education (open schools).

In Madagascar's case, potential target groups are not only students but also teachers, health workers and others where there is a need to upgrade qualifications on a large scale and relatively quickly.

There are three critical success factors for using ODL systems. First, the course must be relevant and useful for the beneficiaries and lead to a meaningful qualification or certificate, accepted by the education system and/or employers. This means ensuring quality and equivalence with formal programs. Without this, programs run the risk of being seen as inferior education and will face poor demand. Second, to operate on a large scale (not as experimental or narrowly targeted programs) the business model must be based on the system becoming self-financing over a period of a few years—this not only leads to sustainability but ensures that there is pressure on managers to reduce costs and be demand-oriented. The selection of appropriate delivery mechanisms and technology platforms are critical. Third, a proper governance structure and professional management are required.

Advances in technology and the operation of large ODL programs in many countries have made it possible to operate such programs in low income countries with limited infrastructure. The availability of learning resources at different levels, which can be procured off the shelf, licensed or as open source material, (often in different languages) has reduced one barrier—the high developmental costs of courses. Models operating in other countries can be adapted easily, paying attention to the replicability of the design features.

---

16. The terms *open learning* and *distance education* represent approaches that focus on opening access to education and training provision, freeing learners from the constraints of time and place, and offering flexible learning opportunities to individuals and groups of learners (UNESCO 2002).

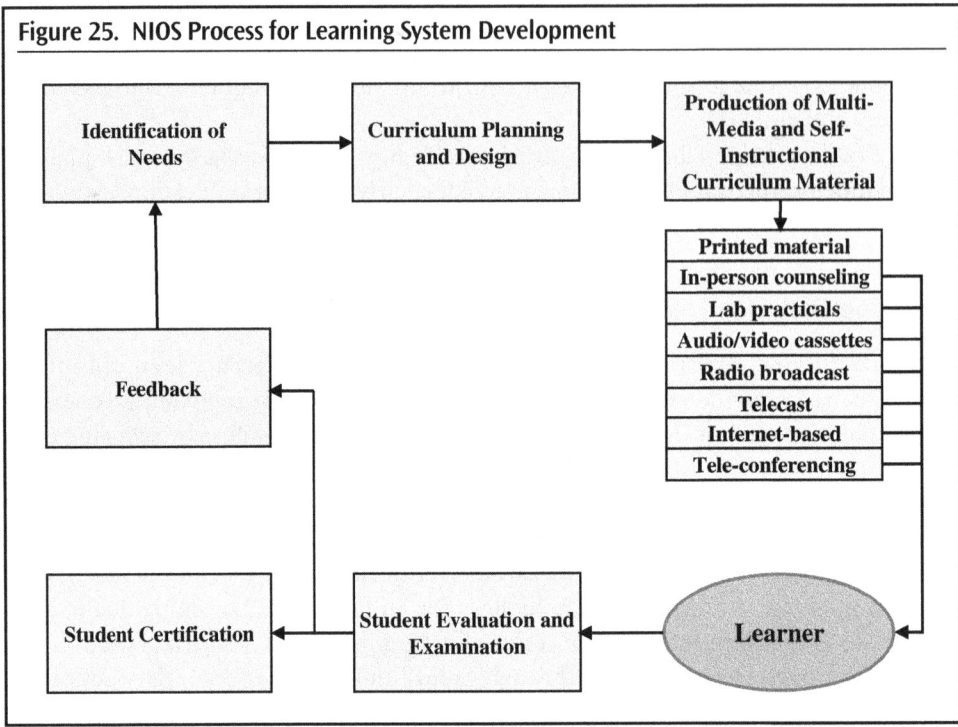

Figure 25. NIOS Process for Learning System Development

Source: Adapted from NIOS website (www.nos.org).

School Education

A variety of approaches are available incorporating different types of technology and delivery systems. Technology varies from correspondence, educational TV and radio, multi-media systems and internet-based systems. Delivery systems either focus on community-based models or school-based models, although the latter is more appropriate for senior secondary education.

The National Institute of Open Schooling in India (NIOS), the largest open school system in the world enrolling 2 million students, provides insights for designing and delivering programs. Its main mission is to provide education and training to school dropouts and marginalized groups through a flexible system of open schooling that is an alternative to formal secondary education. Figure 25 illustrates the structure of NIOS' learning system. NIOS stays flexible by identifying the needs of a given student group, designing interactive curriculum targeted to those needs, evaluating student learning, and feeding evaluation back into curriculum design, to further refine the curriculum.

While the school's early focus was to provide secondary level education, it has extended its range from elementary to senior secondary levels, both academic and vocational. It now operates through ten regional centers and 3000 study centers in India and abroad, providing education in six languages with plans to expand to all 18 official languages (Box 4).

> **Box 4. Main Features of the National Institute of Open School, India**
>
> *Flexible structure.* NIOS provides flexibility in the choice of subjects/courses, place of learning, and transfer of credits from CBSE and State Open Schools to enable the learner's continuation in studies. A learner is given as many as nine chances to appear in public examinations spread over a period of five years. The credits gained are accumulated till the learner clears the required number of credits for certification.
>
> *Variety of learning strategies.* The open schooling programs of NIOS are a mix of traditional system of face-to-face learning with substantial non-traditional inputs such as well designed self-instructional materials, audio-video programs (in both broadcast and non-broadcast modes), video-conferencing/teleconferencing, films and audio programs covering curricular areas, counseling by tutors during Personal Contact Programs and assessment through Tutor Marked Assignments. In addition, curriculum based audio and video programs in Science, Mathematics, Social Science, Hindi, English, etc., for Secondary, Senior Secondary and Vocational Education courses have also been developed for use by learners. The Secondary Education course material of NIOS is available both in print form and on the Internet for use by other students and interested learners. A priced CD version is also available.
>
> *Self-financing.* The NOIS which received funding from the Government of India and technical assistance from the Commonwealth of Learning is now self-financing, relying on student fees. The printed materials published by NIOS for the students are not priced. Their production cost is built into the student fee structure.
>
> *Source:* Prasad, 2007.

Apart from education for school children, the use of ODL for teacher training has now become widespread. Primary school teachers in Brazil without pre-service qualifications are provided training through the national distance education system, PROFORMAÇÃO. The program combines self-study and bi-weekly workshops using print-based and video materials.

Tertiary Level

Worldwide, ODL programs are the most popular at the tertiary level, where students are able to engage in self-directed learning to a greater extent. Following the success of the Open University of Britain, many countries (including developing countries) have followed the model of a single mode university using integrated multimedia systems.

The creation of an open university or modern ODL programs in existing universities is under active consideration in Madagascar. A new initiative to provide distance education through the Francophone Universities Agency is being discussed. Feasibility studies should be undertaken to decide on the programs, learners, delivery mechanisms, technology platforms and business model. It may be appropriate to start programs in areas where delivery can be cost-effective, e.g. business studies, MBA, languages, accounting etc. Various studies have highlighted the ten characteristics of successful Open Universities and the options considered in Madagascar should be evaluated against these criteria (Box 5).

Box 5. Ten Characteristics of Successful Open Universities

1. Organizational mission
   - Clarity of objectives
   - Communicated to the public at large
   - Strong political backing
2. Programs and course curriculum
   - Should enable students to use their learning for career and social mobility
   - Ensure program and curriculum equivalence or validation by the education system/employers
3. Teaching strategies and techniques
   - Largely determined by the course curriculum, economics and the availability of delivery vehicles
   - Science and technology courses will require laboratories and workshops for students to perform hands-on tasks
   - Technology should not exclude groups that may not have access (e.g. television and computer-based learning systems may not be widely available)
4. Learning materials and resources
   - The most important element in an open learning system
   - Choices regarding the process of development are critical (e.g. in-house and centralized course creation, development and production processes; dispersal of various components to institutional and/or commercial agents; or acquisition of ready made learning materials)
   - Acquisition of adaptation of materials is becoming cost-effective due to high cost of course development and variety of specialized skills required
   - Ownership and quality should rest with delivering institution to ensure accountability
5. Communication interaction
   - Effective and timely communication between student and institution on information, counseling, advice on courses and programs, on tuition, examinations etc
   - Students identify strongly with their school, increasing retention
6. Local support systems for learners
   - Provide access to tutor/mentor, library (and labs for science and technology courses) and opportunities for interaction with other students
7. Delivery systems
   - Mechanisms must be established to have the course in the hands or screens of the learner on time and as previously informed or scheduled
   - Use of the public broadcast media, the electronic highway or postal services has to be pre-arranged long before launching
8. Tutorial assistance
   - Careful selection, training and monitoring of course tutors
   - Assessment of workload where tutors are part-time
9. Staffing
   - Different skill mix from the faculty of a traditional tertiary institution
   - Less full-time academics and more administrative staff
   - Traditional academics need training before they can become effective ODL instructors
10. Management and administration
    - Committed leadership, effective management, sensible and efficient administration

Source: Adapted from UNESCO, 2002.

Expanding Private Sector Provision[17]

The private sector has grown rapidly since 1996, with the most rapid growth at the senior secondary level. In 2006/07, the share of private sector in SSE was 54 percent, compared to 39 percent at JSE, and 64 percent in TVET. The private sector share in higher education enrollment was close to 8 percent (Figures 26a and 26b). Private institutions are heavily concentrated in a few districts, notably around the capital of Antananarivo. However, at the senior secondary level, there is much greater regional dispersion. In all regions, they serve mostly urban populations. Seventy percent of JSE institutions (and a similar share of students) are located in urban areas. Almost 85 percent of private SSE institutions are in urban areas (Figure 26).

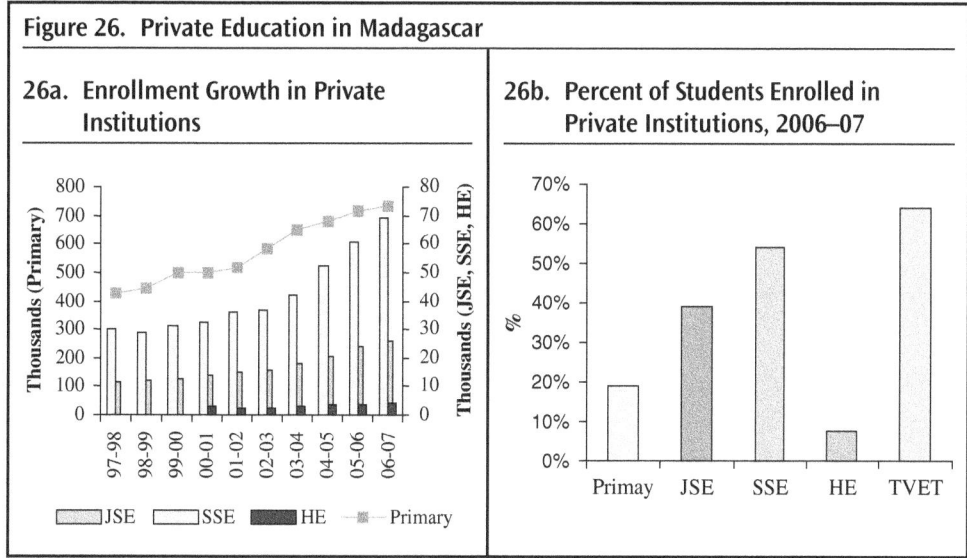

Figure 26. Private Education in Madagascar

26a. Enrollment Growth in Private Institutions

26b. Percent of Students Enrolled in Private Institutions, 2006–07

Source: MEN.
Note: TVET data is for 2005.

Despite these impressive shares in enrollment, the number of private institutions is relatively few—332 SSE schools, 350 TVET schools and only 21 tertiary level institutions. This partly reflects the overall small enrollment size in these sub-sectors. By contrast, there are 5,300 primary schools and over 1,100 junior secondary schools in the private sector, indicating that there is a potential for growth if demand exists and conditions for supply are created.

Programs

Most establishments in school education offer several levels of education from pre-primary to SSE, although technical education is rarely offered. Formally, there is no difference

---

17. This section covers both school education and tertiary education. However, more data are available on secondary education both from the MEN official statistics and from a study financed jointly by World Bank and Agence Francaise de Developpement (d'Aiglepierre, 2008). The study covered school education, for which a survey of junior secondary schools was conducted. However, as most schools have both JSE and SSE, the results are broadly indicative of private secondary education. There has been no detailed study of private tertiary institutions.

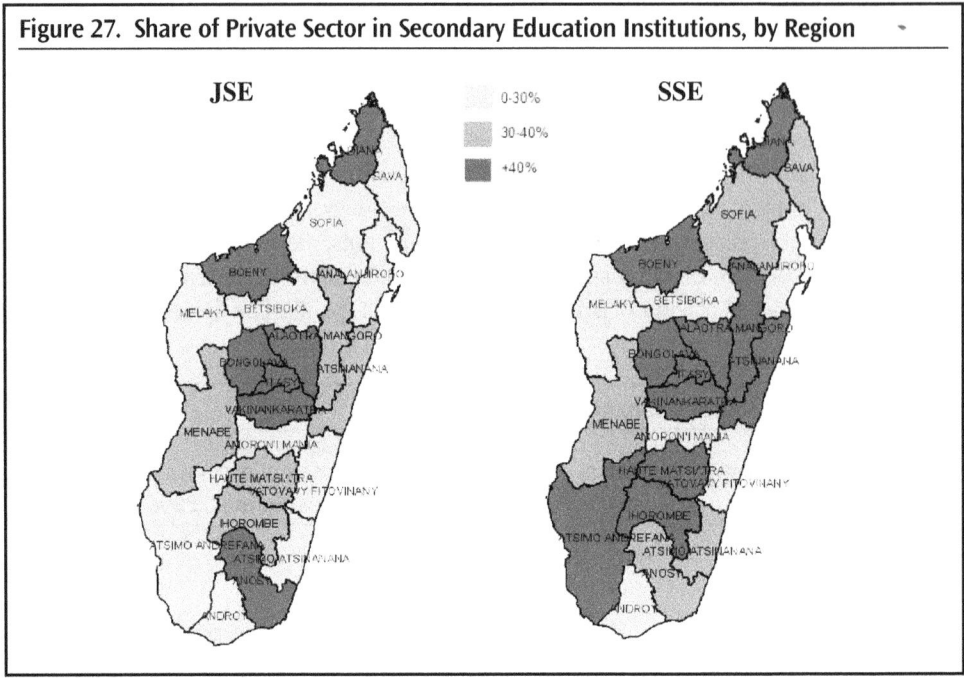

Figure 27. Share of Private Sector in Secondary Education Institutions, by Region

Source: D'Aiglepierre, 2008

in the academic programs in school education between public and private institutions. Madagascar has a single unique curriculum, apart from differences in religious instruction provided in those affiliated to various churches. One appeal of the private sector is that most institutions are able to provide better teaching in French. This is the language of instruction in public schools as well (from grade 3), but most teachers are unable to communicate in French.[18] As in many other countries, private TVET concentrates on lower-cost fields of study oriented towards the services. Private higher education institutions concentrate on job-oriented programs at the *Bac+2* level in a number of fields.

Religious Affiliation

In school education, the private sector consists of a variety of religious institutions and some lay schools. The most important are the Catholic schools, accounting for 44 percent of students, followed by non-affiliated lay schools, accounting for 16 percent. Protestant schools are 7 percent and Lutheran accounts for 3 percent of schools (Figure 28).

School Size

Private JSE and SSE schools tend to be smaller than public institutions. Against an average enrollment size of 342 and 477 in public JSE and SSE, respectively, the size of private JSE

---

18. Under the new EFA program, Malagasy will be the language of instruction from grades 1 to 5.

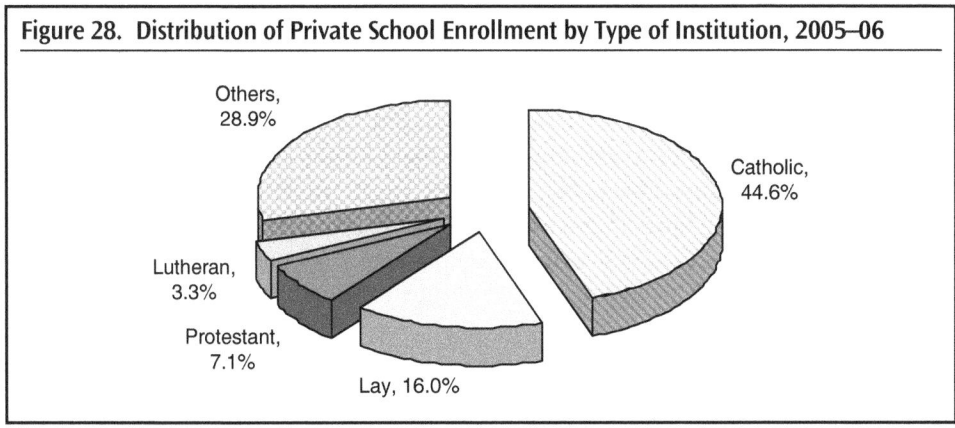

Figure 28. Distribution of Private School Enrollment by Type of Institution, 2005–06

Source: D'Aiglepierre, 2008.

and SSE institutions was 212 and 182, respectively. Because both private and public secondary schools tend to be located in urban areas, competition has led to a reduction in size.

Teachers

Private schools also have significantly lower pupil-teacher ratios; 23 at JSE (compared to 32 in public) and 16 in SSE (compared to 20 in public). However, most teachers are temporary, usually drawn from public schools and teach in multiple institutions. Teachers tend to have higher qualifications but most do not have teacher training. They also receive significantly less in-service training than their public counterparts.[19]

The greater use of polyvalent teachers and longer hours of teaching in private schools represents one important contrast with government schools. Over 50 percent of teachers in private schools teach more than one subject, compared to less than 40 percent in public schools, but public school teachers teach more classes. Private school teachers work on average 10 hours more than their public school counterparts. Almost forty percent of private school teachers work in more than one school. As a result, although public teachers' salaries are about 1.5 times higher than those of private school teachers, total monthly earnings are about comparable.

Demand for Private Education[20]

Who chooses private schools and for what reason? As stated earlier, private education in Madagascar is essentially the same as public education in terms of curriculum and language of institutions, unlike in other countries. The survey found that parents in private school tend to be more educated and on average their family income is higher at 25 percent. However, this is mainly in urban areas. In rural areas, there do not seem to be significant differences in the family income. The main difference is in occupation—private school

---

19. Based on the findings from the World Bank-AFD study and survey results.
20. Based on the findings from the World Bank-AFD study and survey results.

families occupy senior positions in the administration or are businessmen and self-employed. The choice of private schools is sometimes made before grade 1 particularly among richer families, but the majority seems to choose after grade 5. Almost two-thirds of students switch from public to private schools after grade 5. About half the schools report selection exams. Cost is an important element for those choosing public schools. For those choosing private urban schools, perceived quality of teaching and infrastructure are important reasons. However, there may be other reasons; private schools offer longer hours of teaching (about 31–33 in private, compared to 29 in public) and teacher absenteeism is reportedly lower.

Private Costs

At JSE level, the annual cost is estimated to be between 1.8 to 2.8 times higher than public education. On average, at the JSE level, lay institutions are the most costly for families; an average required expenditure of about US$115, compared to US$ 75 in religious institutions and US$ 40 in public. About one-fifths to one-half of this is due to the costs at the beginning of the year, which seems to be the biggest hurdle for parents.

Examination Results

The *baccalauréat* pass rate in private senior secondary schools is similar to that of public schools, but with greater variability across schools. Public secondary schools have higher quality teachers and there is greater competition to enter them, allowing them to choose better students. Without data on student learning, however, it is difficult to assess the relative performance of public and private schools. There are few differences in exam pass rates between public and private schools. Only 50 percent of students pass the JSE certificate in both types of schools.

Constraints on Growth of Private Education

The recent survey of private secondary schools revealed that ownership of land and buildings is the most important factor in deciding the location of a private secondary school. About two-thirds of private secondary schools either own the land or have free use of it (the land could be by owned the proprietor or religious institutions). Purchasing of land is not easy, partly due to the cost but also because land titles are not clear and related legal issues. Another important constraint is access to credit. The average capital requirement to start a private junior secondary school is about 20 million Ariary (about US$10,000), including average cost of buildings, land, and start-up costs. Almost all of this is financed by personal savings of the founder or contributions from religious institutions, parents or foreign patrons. The use of credit from banks or micro finance institutions is negligible. Even when they did take it, for most the loan size was less than US$2,500. Both these constraints—land and access and cost of credit—are common for all businesses.

A variety of public subsidies are provided for private schools. Private schools receive five types of transfers, which are summarized in Table 3. The transfers lack clear objectives

Table 3. Types of Public Financing for Private Schools

Subsidy	Level of education	Objective	Unit cost	Criteria for eligibility/ disbursement	Number of beneficiaries
1. Teachers' salary	Primary, JSE, SSE	Encourage teachers to obtain certificate	20,000 Ariary/ teacher/year (US$10)	Teachers with certificate. Distributed by CISCO.	18,200 teachers
2. School contracts	Primary, JSE, SSE	Improve performance	Amounts vary	School development plan, approved by CISCO/Regional Directions.	100 schools
3. School fee reduction	Primary	Free primary education	270,000 Ariary/ teacher/yr (US$135)	Schools with fees below US$1 per month	4,300 schools
4. School grants	Primary	Universal free primary education	US$1 per student	All private primary schools	All primary schools
5. Subsidy to private school organizations (*Directions Nationales*)	Primary, JSE, SSE	To support administrative costs	5 cents per enrolled child	All recognized national organizations of private schools (percentage of total transfers)	

Note: Amounts in dollars are approximate using an exchange rate of US$1 = 2000 Ariary.
Source: Adapted from d'Aiglepierre, 2008.

and are subject to arbitrary changes. This reflects a lack of a coherent policy framework for private education and creates uncertainties for private operators. Examples of repeated policy changes include:

- *Subsidies for teachers' salaries:* a nominal amount of US$10 per teacher is given to private school teachers with a certificate to teach. The policy underwent many changes after its institution in 1996. It was suspended between 2000 and 2002, taken up in 2003, suspended in 2004 and 2005, and reinstated in 2006.
- *School contracts:* Provides funding for pedagogical activities to schools with an agreed contract to deliver results. School contracts were suspended in 2003 and re-instated in 2006. The coverage is very low.
- *School grants for primary private schools:* Compensates for abolition of fees and purchase school supplies. Instituted since 2003.
- *Subsidy to national organizations of private schools:* Supports administrative costs. Has increased between 2000 and 2006, but is very low.

In total, the subsidies to the private sector account for about 3 percent of total non-personnel recurrent spending of the Ministry. This relatively small amount is fragmented into different channels with little impact. There are no subsidies for private higher education institutions.

Regulatory Framework

The legal framework recognizes the right of private education and private institutions are free to set fee levels and salaries of teachers. Private schools can be established after receiving three authorizations: (i) the school infrastructure satisfies minimum criteria stated in the rules (ii) the principal meets qualification criteria and (iii) the teaching personnel has the requisite qualifications at each level. At the SSE level, this means that the principal must have the teaching certificate for at least three years and that teachers have completed the first level of university studies (Bac +2). Applications to open a school is usually submitted to the district head for primary schools, the regional head for junior secondary schools and the national office for senior secondary schools (*Office Nationales de l'Enseignement Privé*—ONEP) for senior secondary schools. Authorizations regarding the principal and teaching staff have to be requested from the district or regional head.

The regulatory framework at the school level appears relatively clear and simple. Authorizations for secondary schools are supposed to be given in 3 months. Nevertheless, about 12 percent of schools operate without receiving formal approval, apparently because their applications are rejected due to lack of information. Better communication of the procedures and training of district and regional staff should help overcome such problems.

Obligations of private schools include maintaining the legal documents, the student register and an annual report to ONEP about student enrollment, teachers, financial data and use of subsidies. However, there is no regular monitoring or assessment of the quality of private schools.

In contrast to school education, both in higher education and in technical/vocational education, the policy and regulatory framework is unclear and inconsistently applied. A request for opening a new private institution requires a visit to the premises and verification that norms are adhered to. A provisional authorization is given for 2 years, after which an evaluation is done and a permanent authorization is given. However, there is no accreditation although the institutions offer state approved programs. In practice, there are many delays in approval by the Ministry of Education, causing institutions to seek approval from the Ministry of Labor, which also has the authority to approve.

In higher education, two types of recognition are given: simple authority to open an institution and "*homologation*" (approval). There is no accreditation or quality assurance system. However, since 2002, "*homologation*" has been suspended and since 2005, no new authorization to open HEI has been granted. The number of institutions has stagnated as a result, although the existing institutions continue to expand enrollments. The Ministry recognizes the need to update its procedures for recognition and to introduce accreditation and has prepared draft criteria, using World Bank funded technical assistance. However, action has been pending on these measures.

Measures to Increase Private Provision

Using the private sector to expand provision especially in urban areas is a sensible policy choice, allowing the government to concentrate its resources on improving access for underserved areas and groups. In school education, the existence of a reasonable regulatory framework means that this can advance fairly quickly. Effort should be focused on (i) clarifying and communicating the procedures (ii) rationalizing the subsidy programs for SSE (as well as JSE) and creating school development funds and/or scholarship programs with transparent eligibility criteria and well-designed implementation mechanisms and (iii) building capacity at the central and local levels to implement the programs.

In TVET and higher education, priority should be given to finalize and approve the procedures for recognition and accreditation. Further technical assistance will be required to design the institutional mechanisms and build up capacity. A more detailed study of private institutions in these two sub-sectors, to identify additional constraints, should also be undertaken.

CHAPTER 6

Partnerships for Growth

Innovation and On-the-Job Training

Despite a few outstanding examples, neither Madagascar's tertiary institutions nor its firms have played a significant role in promoting applied innovation or workforce development. As a result, Madagascar is failing to capitalize on its potential to increase productivity through development and manufacture of higher value-add goods.

This chapter will describe and explore the expanded role that tertiary institutions and private firms could play in making Madagascar more productive. Organized by section, the chapter will present how Madagascar ranks against other countries today; what investments in innovation and workforce development are today; and how these investments might be enhanced through public intervention.

Current Status: Global Competitiveness and Innovation

Madagascar's Comparative Position

Madagascar ranks very low on international indices of competitiveness and knowledge. The Global Competitiveness Index (GCI), which ranks countries on the conditions considered essential to economic growth, ranked Madagascar 118 out of 131 countries in 2007.[21]

---

21. The GCI uses two types of data: (i) data from the Executive Opinion Survey administered by the WEF and (ii) hard data. The former comprises qualitative information based on subjective assessments; the latter relates to quantitative data collected from international organizations. Of the 113 variables making up the index, approximately two thirds come from the Executive Opinion Survey, and one third comes from publicly available sources.

This is not surprising in itself, nor unusual in comparison to other low income countries in sub-Saharan Africa. It does suggest that Madagascar's current tools for driving gains in productivity are limited.

However, change is possible. Madagascar's ranks 35th on the time required to start a business, reflecting the progress that Madagascar has made in simplifying procedures since the last GCI rating in 2005.

Higher Education and Training

Low Performance on GCI. Madagascar's higher education and training system is poor quality. The GCI is structured around a series of sub-indexes and pillars (Table 4). Of the pillars, Madagascar ranks near-bottom on "higher education and training" (121), trailed only by "financial market sophistication" (123).

Table 4. Madagascar's Global Competitiveness Index Rankings, 2007–08	
	Rank
Overall (out of 131)	118
Sub-index A: Basic requirements	120
1st pillar: Institutions	93
2nd pillar: Infrastructure	115
3rd pillar: Macroeconomic stability	118
4th pillar: Health and primary education	106
Sub-index B: Efficiency enhancers	121
5th pillar: Higher education and training	121
6th pillar: Goods market efficiency	105
7th pillar: Labor market efficiency	63
8th pillar: Financial market sophistication	123
9th pillar: Technological readiness	111
10th pillar: Market size	104
Sub-index C: Innovation and sophistication	94
11th pillar: Business sophistication	104
12th pillar: Innovation	84

Source: World Economic Forum, 2008.

Rankings within each sub-index reveal the indicators that contribute to the extremely low ranking on higher education and training (Table 5). Madagascar ranks poorly on secondary and tertiary enrollment rates, internet access in schools, the availability of specialized research and training services, the extent of staff training and the quality of the overall educational system. The quality of math and science education, the quality of management schools, and the availability of scientists and engineers have relatively higher rankings.

Table 5. Madagascar's GCI Rankings for Higher Education and Training, 2007

Pillar/Sub-indicator	Rank (1 = high, 131 = low)
Higher education and training pillar	121
Secondary enrollment (hard data)	126
Tertiary enrollment (hard data)	121
Internet access in schools	116
Local availability of specialized research and training services	108
Extent of staff training	107
Quality of the educational system	101
Quality of math and science education	83
Quality of management schools	74
Quality of math and science education	83
Quality of management schools	74

Source: World Economic Forum, 2008.

Innovation

Higher Performance on GCI. By contrast, Madagascar's innovation ranking is better (84). The ranking is due to relatively strong performance (below 100) on all innovation-related sub-indicators but one—the quality of scientific research institutions (Table 6). These rankings suggest that Madagascar has some innovation strengths that it can build upon: university-industry research collaboration, innovation capacity, patenting, company spending on R&D, availability of scientists and engineers, and government procurement of advanced technology.

Table 6. Madagascar's GCI Rankings for Innovation, 2007

Pillar/Sub-indicator	Rank (1 = high, 131 = low)
Innovation pillar	84
Quality of scientific research institutions	106
University-industry research collaboration	96
Capacity for innovation	91
Utility patents (hard data)	89
Company spending on R&D	86
Availability of scientists and engineers	62
Government procurement of advanced technology products	53

Source: World Economic Forum, 2008.

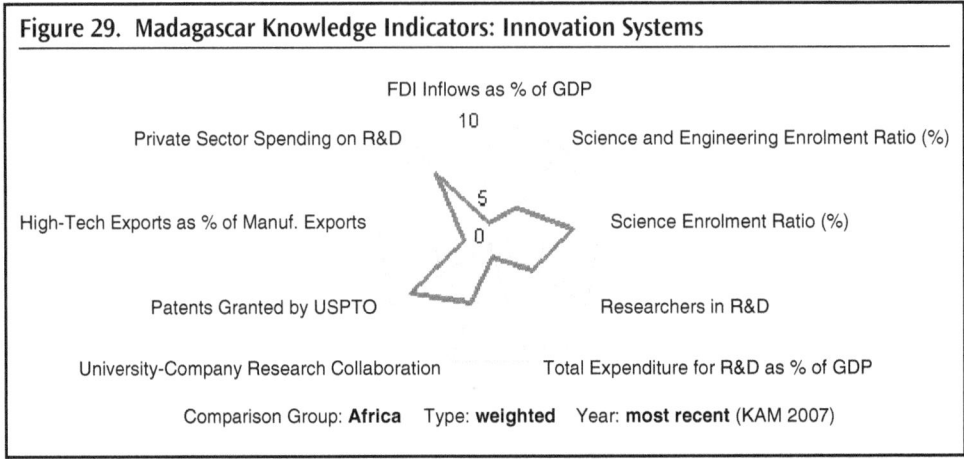

Figure 29. Madagascar Knowledge Indicators: Innovation Systems

Source: World Bank Knowledge Assessment Methodology (KAM) website (www.worldbank.org/kam).

Relatively Good Performance on "Knowledge Economy Index." Innovation indicators from the World Bank's Knowledge Economy Index reinforce the GCI conclusion that Madagascar has innovation strengths that it can build upon. Figure 29 shows Madagascar's performance on innovation-related indicators, relative to SSA countries overall.[22] While FDI inflows and high-tech exports as percentage of manufacturing exports are low, science enrollment ratio, patents granted by the United States Patents and Trademarks Office (USPTO), and private sector spending on research and development (R&D) are relatively high.

In comparison with South Africa and Mauritius, two middle income African countries, Figure 30 show that Madagascar still does well on the science enrollment ratio, the quality of science and math education, and private sector spending on R&D.

Modest Performance on Firm-level Innovation. Data from the Investment Climate Assessment (ICA) survey of 2005 provide insights into innovation at the firm level in the formal sector, reported in Table 7. These insights are complementary to those suggested by the GCI and KEI indices.

Madagascar's firms did not innovate on a significant scale. Spending on R&D was higher in Madagascar than in other low income SSA countries, at 0.4 percent of sales. At the same time, only about a third of firms introduced new production technology, and less than 10 percent had ISO certification. For over three-quarters of firms, procuring new machinery—a less sophisticated approach to driving innovation—was the most important means of acquiring new technology. Less than 7 percent of firms reported other ways of upgrading technologies, such as hiring new technically qualified personnel, licensing technology, or using turnkey projects and developing in-house technology. No firm reported acquiring technology from universities or public institutions (not reported in table).

---

22. The index uses 140 indicators to measure the performance of countries on the four Knowledge Economy (KE) pillars: Economic Incentive and Institutional Regime, Education, Innovation, and Information and Communications Technologies. The index is the simple average of the normalized country scores on key variables. The diagrams demonstrate *comparative performance*—the variables are normalized on a scale from 0 to 10 relevant to comparison groups. The normalization procedure can be found on the Knowledge Assessment Methodology website.

Figure 30. Select Knowledge Indicators: Madagascar and Middle-income SADC Countries

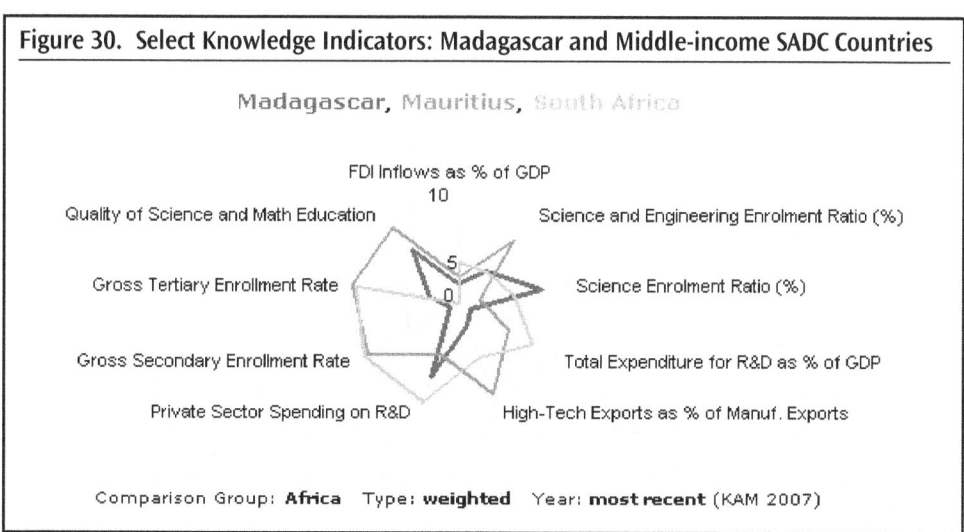

Source: World Bank Knowledge Assessment Methodology (KAM) website (www.worldbank.org/kam).

Table 7. Innovation Indicators for Madagascar's Formal Sector Manufacturing Firms, 2005

Country	Year	ISO certification ownership	Technology licensed from foreign company	New production technology	New product or substantial upgrade of existing product	Spending on R&D (% sales)	New machinery	Hiring key personnel	Licensing/turnkey operations	Joint ventures
AVERAGE	ALL	14	14	37	64	0.5	62	8	4	20
Benin	2004	3	4	..	62	0.6	64	6	2	19
Eritrea	2002	7	..	..	..	0.2	..	..	..	..
Ethiopia	2002	2	..	..	..	0.1	33	14	3	32
Kenya	2003	..	8	..	..	0.3	39	4	6	25
Madagascar	2005	7	8	37	66	0.4	77	7	2	7
Mali	2003	7	10	50	66	0.7	62	5	2	12
Mauritius	2005	28	24	62	72	2.3	73	6	4	13
Senegal	2003	6	15	..	..	..	75	3	2	16
South Africa	2003	42	23	61	89	0.5	25	8	11	39
Tanzania	2003	12	16	32	63	1.1	36	13	1	35
Uganda	2003	..	..	47	..	..	66	6	3	18
Zambia	2002	6	8	50	78	0.2	24	10	9	32

Source: World Bank, Enterprise surveys website (www.enterprisesurveys.org).

In sum, Madagascar has some good building blocks for innovation. These include strong enrollment in relatively good quality math and science education, a relatively high number of patented innovations, and a relatively high level of private investment in R&D (although at less than one percent, this level is still very low when compared to R&D investments for firms in high income countries). At the same time, Malagasy firms struggle to translate innovation potential into the development and sale of higher-value goods and services. The "policy directions" section of this chapter will explore ways that public intervention can drive more productive research and development.

Current Status: Investments in Innovation and Training

Innovation in Tertiary Institutions

Madagascar has low levels of innovation in tertiary institutions, for two primary reasons. First, and as will be highlighted in the following chapter, Madagascar devotes few public resources to R&D. Its 2007 expenditure for scientific research was 4 percent of the $65.5M public education budget. Most visibly, the low level of funding results in a lack of research facilities, equipment and doctoral level graduates (just over 380). There is also little funding for research projects, which results in low rates of faculty publication (in 2005, just one percent of the faculty published in academic journals) and, consequently, little of the knowledge transfer required to spur innovation.

Second, incentives are not structured to encourage universities or faculty to undertake serious research. There is not a clear regulatory framework for research. Without a clear view of how proceeds from research would be divided, neither researchers nor universities have a strong incentive to undertake research. Moreover, many faculty members supplement their university salaries by teaching additional hours in universities and/or in private institutions. When faced with the decision to pursue research (for which there is little funding or potential for financial reward) or augment their income, many university professors make the reasonable choice to increase their income.

Firm-based Workforce Training

Malagasy firms make modest investments in work-force training, especially in larger firms and for managers, other professionals, and those with higher levels of education. However, given positive returns to productivity, it appears that Malagasy firms still underinvest in training. This section reviews the nature of firm-based workforce training, as highlighted in the 2005 ICA survey, as well as the returns to training.

Incidence of Training. Employee training in the formal manufacturing sector seems quite extensive. About 48 percent of enterprises reported having organized internal or external training in the year preceding the survey (i.e., 2004). This was higher than the average of 40 percent for the region and significantly higher than, for example, firms in South Asia. The incidence of training was significantly higher in large firms (100 employees or more), with nearly over three-quarters of firms providing some kind of training. At the other end of the spectrum, 32 percent of small firms (fewer than 20 employees) provided training.

Training Intensity. Relatively few workers received training. About 27 percent of workers in firms that provided training benefited from training. Overall, less than 10 percent of all permanent skilled workers in the sample received any training (compared to 22 percent for the region). Thus, while a larger proportion of firms seem to provide training compared to other countries, the training deficit is large in terms of the relatively few numbers who are trained. Training appears to be concentrated on managers and professionals.

Sources of Training. About 24 percent of firms provided internal training, 12 percent provide external training, and 13 percent provided both. The incidence of external training was particularly low in small firms where only 10 percent provided external training, compared to over 50 percent among large firms. Data are not available on what types of training institutes were used (domestic public and private, or foreign). A study of the textile and garment industry indicated that many firms, particularly foreign firms operating in the export processing zones, tend to send middle level managers and professionals abroad for training.

Determinants of Training. The determinants of training can be analyzed by using a logistic model in which the indicator variable—whether a firm offers any training—is regressed on a set of explanatory variables. The marginal effects show the effects of a unit change in one of the explanatory variables on the probability that a firm will train, calculated at the average value of the explanatory variables.[23] The variables that have the highest, statistically significant impact on the probability of training are: whether the firm is large, whether it is innovative, the average education level of workers, and its capital intensity. Firms in the textile and apparel industry and in chemicals and pharmaceuticals are also more likely to provide training (Table 8).

These findings are consistent with empirical results from other countries. Firms that use more capital per worker tend to be technology-intensive and require workers with appropriate skills created by training. Large firms tend to have more managerial capabilities and may also be able to access training at lower cost. They are also able to invest in training without fear of losing trained workers to competitors. Firm-based training is complementary to education because educated workers tend to benefit more from training.

Impact on Productivity. Firms will undertake training only if they benefit through increases in productivity. A production function model can be used to assess the impact on productivity. Annex 2 shows the results of a stochastic production frontier model which regresses value added on a set of explanatory variables such as physical capital, labor (full-time equivalent, permanent, and temporary), the share of female workers, industrial sector, whether the firm introduced innovations, the number of years of education and whether the enterprise provided training. The stock of human capital, as measured by average years of worker education, has a positive impact on firm-level productivity, with a 9 percent rate of return for each year of study. The introduction of the education variable reduces significantly the return on physical capital, and suggests complementarity between physical and human capital (Model 4 in the Annex).

Training of workers is beneficial for firms. Internal training, as measured by an indicator variable (whether the firm provides training or not), has a strong estimated impact,

---

23. For example, for a firm that introduced an innovation, the probability of providing training is about 0.18 higher than for a non-innovation firm. The coefficient itself indicates the log-odds of a firm undertaking training (versus not training); taking the exponent gives the odds of it providing training (versus not providing training).

Table 8. Determinants of the Decision to Train Employees in the Formal Manufacturing Sector, 2004

Dependent variable = Probability of any training	Average	Coefficient	Marginal effect
Capital/worker (10^6)	57.14	0.0013*	0.0003*
Education level of employees (years)	8.22	0.2161**	0.0524**
Firm size (excluded category =small)			
Medium	0.38	0.2579	0.0628
Large	0.22	2.0796***	0.4722***
Innovative firm	0.34	0.7652*	0.1868*
Foreign	0.33	0.4608	0.1127
Exporter	0.22	0.0248	0.0060
Located in export processing zone	0.15	−0.7780	−0.1754
Sector (excluded =agro industry)			
Textiles, apparel	0.30	2.0327***	0.4681***
Wood and furniture	0.23	1.1841*	0.2876
Paper and Printing	0.02	1.5266	0.3529
Chemicals and pharmaceuticals	0.08	1.7162**	0.3927**
Metallurgy and machinery	0.07	0.0026	0.0006
Non-metal and plastic	0.04	0.0173	0.0042
Others	0.13	0.5206	0.1287
Constant		−4.1513	
Pseudo R^2		0.2287	
Number of observations	166		

*** = significant at 1%; ** = significant at 5%; * = significant at 10%; ^ = significant at 20%.

Notes: 1 Logistic model with dependent variable (0.1) showing whether the firm offered any training (internal or external). 2. Marginal effect calculated by the mid-point for continuous variables or for a variation of 0 to 1 discrete variables 3. Innovative firm is one which had introduced new technology for producing a new product or modifying the production process for an existing product in the preceding years.

Source: Lassibille, 2008.

raising productivity by 33 percent (Model 5). External training was not included in the model as it relatively few firms provide this form of training. However, even though training raises productivity, as shown earlier, only some categories of firms are likely to train—large enterprises and innovative firms, among others. Economies of scale in the provision of training may be one reason for this. Smaller firms, which use relatively little physical capital, and those that are using mature technologies do not need to provide workers with additional training and the human capital levels of their workers are also lower.

Impact on Earnings. Enterprise training benefits workers through higher earnings, as well, with an estimated 8 percent rate of return. Hence, training benefits both firms—in terms of productivity gains—and workers—in terms of increased earnings. However, only certain categories of workers benefit: those higher levels of education (Table 9), managers and professionals. Other categories of workers are less likely to receive such training.

Table 9. Determinants of Training and Impact on Earnings, Formal Industry Sector 2005		
Dependent variable = Impact on earnings	Average in the sample	Marginal effect
Effects on the probability of participation in training [a]		
Years of study	12.02	0.004***
Level of education (%)[b]		
General secondary	48.1	0.035**
Technical secondary	9.0	0.0521
Professional secondary	5.7	0.096*
Higher	17.7	0.142**
Occupation (%)[c]		
Skilled production workers	19.1	−0.035***
Unskilled production workers	44.3	−0.082
Non-production workers	26.4	−0.049***
Effect of training on earnings	—	8.00**

Notes: * = significant at 10%; ** = significant at 5%; *** = significant at 1%.
[a] Table summarizes results of various regressions with different model specifications. Data are from workers' module.
[b] Compared to an employee with a level of primary education or less.
[c] Compared to a manager/professional.
Source: Lassibille (2007) analysis of ICA 2005 data.

Reasons for Underinvestment in Training. It appears that Malagasy firms underinvest in training: although training is associated with positive effects on productivity (a benefit to the firm) and on earnings (a benefit to the worker), firms do not invest in training most of their employees.

There are several reasons for which firms are likely to underinvest in workforce development. They will not invest in training unless they will lose their competitive edge by *not* training employees. In many sectors, firms operating with limited capital and low skilled workers, employers perceive that workers won't be able to absorb the training because workers are not educated enough. Most firms use "mature" technologies for which there is little economic surplus to be gained from more training. Further, for small firms, the opportunity costs of sending workers for external training are very high (for example, the entire production can be held up if one out of five workers goes for training). The lack of affordable training and the fear of losing trained workers to competitors can also lead to underinvestment.

For these reasons, although training generates positive and high returns, private decisions may not lead to the optimal level of investment. Public intervention and possibly financing may be required to raise training. The next section of this chapter will suggest policy tools that can be used to encourage firms invest more in employee training.

Policy Directions: Fostering Investment in Innovation and Training

Tertiary Institutions

From a strategic viewpoint, Madagascar must strive to increase the number of researchers and Ph.D. graduates in priority fields. The current annual output of doctoral level graduates (just over 380) is insufficient. An increase in number of researchers and Ph.D.s is necessary, first and foremost, to develop the cadre of qualified university faculty who will improve tertiary level teaching. Priority should be given to the fields in which the Government plans to increase undergraduate enrollment, consistent with its growth objectives. Faculty recruitment policies must also change, as discussed in Chapter 4. A final change would be to link the provision of Ph.D. training to the new faculty recruitment policies and terms. An increase in the number of researchers and Ph.D.s is also necessary to improve the quality of university research. Measures should encourage promising young academics to enter into research. They could include allowing graduates with a Master's degree who show evidence of superior performance and potential to be recruited as researchers, and creation of a "young scholars program" to provide small grants to new Ph.D. graduates to continue their research, with the aim of driving applied innovation in areas of high priority to the economy.

Given Madagascar's relative strengths in research capacity, the government could start actively promoting applied research in select priority areas. Traditional university research has tended to be academic, with the implicit bias of generating "new technologies" through basic research. With the existing poor state of infrastructure and the shortage of qualified researchers, however, generating new technologies is an unrealistic objective for Madagascar. In addition, and as observed above, there is a more pressing need to translate innovation potential into the development and sale of new, higher-value goods and services.

A more productive approach to innovation would be structured around two principles: (i) concentrate on applied research and problem-solving related to production-related problems, and (ii) encourage universities to proactively acquire technology that can be adapted to local conditions. In addition to the formal sector, adaptation of technology should focus on technology for the primary sector (agriculture, horticulture, fisheries, etc).

The policy to promote research and innovation capacity could concentrate on four areas:

1. *Development of young researchers.* Build up a cadre of young researchers in priority fields, through awards for doctoral programs.
2. *Competitive funding of research.* Provide competitive research funds to solve problems that are important for national and regional economic development.
3. *Continual researcher learning.* Ensure that experienced researchers are able to keep up with research methods and latest developments in their field of specialization through workshops and seminars. This component would be linked to the program of faculty development in universities.
4. *Encouragement of contract research.* At the moment, foreign firms operating in Madagascar are more likely to engage in such research, rather than domestic firms. It would be advisable to asses whether foreign firms contract research outside the country and whether Malagasy researchers can engage in contract research. The government could provide matching grants to encourage foreign firms to undertake research in the country.

In order to make this feasible, financing and governance reforms in universities and tertiary level institutions are indispensable. These are discussed in later chapters.

Private Firms

Malagasy firms underinvest in training, even though training is associated with positive effects on productivity and earnings. Further, training is confined largely to big firms, and they rely to a large extent on internal training. When firms resort to external training, institutions outside the country are frequently used.

As outlined previously, the reasons for underinvestment in training appear to be the lack of competitive need to do so; worker difficulty in absorbing training lessons, due to low education levels; use of outdated equipment for which training is not required, nor will yield economic benefit; the lack of affordable training; and the fear of losing trained workers to competitors.

The government can play a major role in counter-acting these incentives by: (i) fostering industry cooperation to boost firm-based training and (ii) enabling domestic education and training institutions to tap into this market. Both these policy measures require setting up appropriate governance mechanisms for employers to express their training needs, participate in designing programs that are relevant for their needs and accredit training providers.

CHAPTER 7

Adapting to Change

Issues and Reforms in Public Expenditure and Finance Management

Improvement of quality and increasing access to pos-basic education will require more resources, public and private. Using those resources efficiently should be a major concern for Madagascar. International experience also indicates that *how* public resources are provided can greatly impact efficiency and quality improvement by changing the behavior of education institutions.

This chapter reviews the trends and composition of public spending on post-basic education, per student expenditures, the drivers of recurrent expenditure and the issues in resource utilization. It reviews the efficiency of budget management and the impact of recent reforms. The chapter concludes with the identification of reform priorities in three areas: better resource utilization, enhanced resource mobilization and reforms in resource allocation mechanisms.

Trends and Composition of Public Spending

Between 2002 and 2006, public spending on education grew by 62 percent, after adjusting for inflation, or 13 percent per annum. While creditable, this increase comes after years of underinvestment and 2002 itself was a year of crisis. Madagascar spent about 2 percent of GDP in 1996, a share which steadily rose to 3.3 percent in 2001, fell to 2.7 percent in 2002 and has by now recovered to its pre-crisis levels. Madagascar's public expenditure effort for education is comparable to that of other low income countries (Figure 31).

Sub-sectoral shares of government education expenditure reveal the priority given to primary education and some protection of junior secondary education, and suggest under-funding of the post-basic levels. In the former, between 2002 and 2006, real

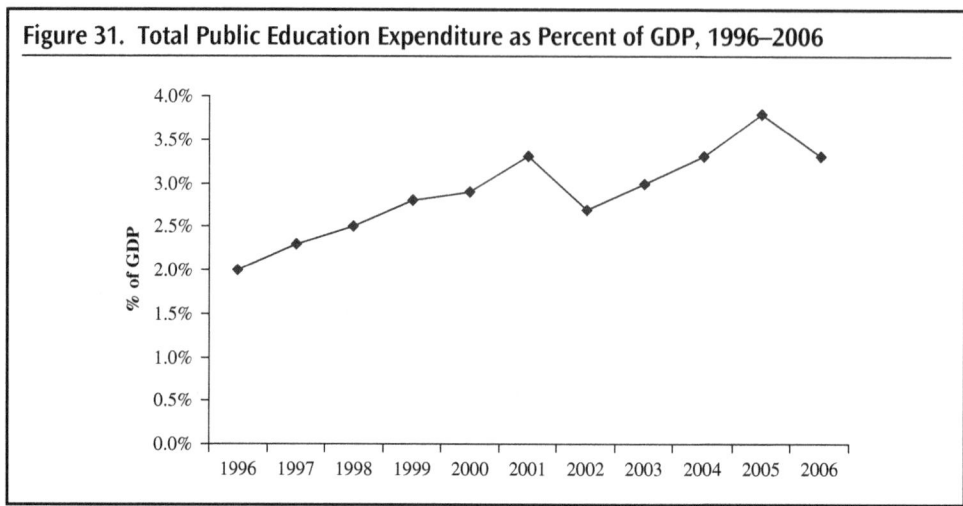

Figure 31. Total Public Education Expenditure as Percent of GDP, 1996–2006

Source: World Bank analysis of MEN data.

spending increased by close to 125 percent; in the latter, by almost 50 percent. Real spending rose in all the other sub-sectors as well, with about 35 percent increase in senior secondary education and higher education and only 10 percent increase in TVET. As a result, the share of primary education in total public expenditure rose from 43 percent to 59 percent. The shares of other sub-sectors declined: in SSE, from 7 percent to 6 percent, in technical/vocational training from 3 percent to 2 percent and in higher education (including scientific research) from 19 percent to 16 percent. The latter is set to decline further to about 13 percent in 2007. Excluding scientific research, higher education receives only 11 percent of the education budget (Table 10).

In relation to GDP, public spending on post-basic education is miniscule. Madagascar spends about 0.4 percent of GDP on higher education (excluding scientific research) and about 0.2 percent on SSE. The former is lower than the average even for francophone SSA countries (0.5 percent) and for Anglophone countries (0.8 percent).

Capital expenditures increased by almost four-fold in real terms between 2002 and 2006. Most of this was for primary education, largely externally financed, and accounts for the increase in the share of this sub-sector. In 2006, for example, of total capital expenditures of 109 billion Ariary, about 98 billion was spent on primary education. These figures are somewhat misleading because a significant part of the "capital expenditures" in primary education includes recurrent expenditures (for example, for remuneration of primary teachers and teacher training).[24] Even with these adjustments, the share of other sub-sectors is extremely low while absolute amounts are small and variable. In 2006, investment in SSE was 2.1 billion Ariary (approx US $ 1 million) and in TVET, 980 million Ariary (US $ 0.5 million). However, investment in higher education and scientific research was sig-

---

24. A part of these are financed by external projects and hence classified as "capital expenditures" in the budget.

Table 10. Allocation of Public Education Expenditure by Sub-sector, 2002–07							
	Share of education by sub-sector						
	2002	2003	2004	2005	2006	2007 (est.)	% real increase, 2002–06
Total Education Exp (billions Ariary current prices)	163	206	266	388	387	463	61.9%
Of which: (%)							
Pre-school	—	—	—	—	—	0.5%	n.a.
Primary	43%	38%	51%	57%	59%	55%	124%
JSE	11%	14%	10%	11%	10%	10%	48%
SSE (incl tech. ed)	7%	6%	4%	6%	6%	5%	36%
TVET	3%	3%	3%	3%	2%	2%	11%
Higher Education	16%	10%	10%	10%	13%	11%	35%
Scientific Research	3%	7%	2%	3%	3%	2%	65%
Administration	18%	23%	19%	11%	8%	14%	(32%)
Memo Items:							
Total in US $ million	119	166	142	194	181	247	
Exchange Rate (1 US$)	1366	1238	1869	2003	2142	1874	

Notes: 1. Total expenditure represents executed budget (commitment basis) and includes recurrent and capital expenditure. 2. 2007 data are provisional. 3. Real increase calculated using inflation-adjusted expenditures by sub-sector and for total. 4. Education total in parentheses are in current prices.
Sources: 1. For 2002–2005, MEN, 2008b. *Rapport d'Etat du Système Educatif National Malgache.* 2. For 2006 and 2007, MEN. 2008a. *Mise en œuvre du plan Éducation Pour Tous–Bilan annuel 2007.* Annex 1. 3. Exchange rates from World Bank Global Development Finance online database.

nificantly greater at 7.9 billion Ariary (approximately US$ 3.6 million), but this was mostly due to expenditure on scientific research, financed by external projects in other sectors. Investment in higher education institutions has been in the range of US $ 2–4 million per year between 2002 and 2006 (Table 11).

Capital expenditures are largely financed by external sources and this explains the high share of primary education and negligible shares for other sub-sectors. Donors have provided funding almost exclusively for primary education: in 2006, donor funding for education was 68 billion Ariary, or about 10 times the funding to all other education levels combined. Scientific research receives a higher share of total capital expenditures than higher education for the same reason (Figure 32).[25] With a high level of dependence on donor funding in the education sector, budget allocations reflect donor priorities to a great extent. The domestic investment budget is too small to make a significant impact on changing sub-sectoral priorities.

---

25. In 2006, an IDA project on rural development accounted for the bulk of R & D investment expenditure; in 2007, the major share was due to the National Program on Nutrition financed by UNICEF.

Table 11. Allocation of Public Capital Expenditures in Education by Sub-sector, 2002–07

	Share of capital expenditure					
	2002	2003	2004	2005	2006	2007
Total Capital Exp (billions Ar current)	27	49	69	123	109	123
Of which (in %):						
Pre-school	—	—	—	—	—	2%
Primary	15%	15%	69%	81%	90%	86%
JSE	2%	2%	3%	3%	0.3%	2%
SSE	3%	1%	0%	3%	2%	4%
TVET	3%	1%	1%	0.9%	0.1%	0.4%
Higher Education	22%	5%	5%	7%	1%	0.9%
Scientific Research	9%	24%	3%	5%	6%	4%
Administration	47%	52%	18%	0%	0.7%	1%
Total in US $ mill.	19.7	40.0	37.0	61.6	51.0	65.5

Notes: 1. Executed budget (commitment basis). 2. 2007 data are provisional.
Sources: 1. For 2002–2005, MEN, 2008b. *Rapport d'Etat du Système Educatif National Malgache.* 2. For 2006 and 2007, MEN. 2008a. *Mise en œuvre du plan Éducation Pour Tous–Bilan annuel 2007.* Annex 1. 3. Exchange rates from World Bank Global Development Finance online database.

The increase in real public recurrent expenditures has just kept pace with enrollment in SSE and higher education (Table 12). In TVET, per student unit expenditure declined by about 25 percent between 2002 and 2006, mainly due to increase in the student: teacher ratio. In dollar terms, the unit expenditure in SSE, TVET and higher education was about US$180, US$206 and US$570 in 2006. These low absolute values reflect primarily low

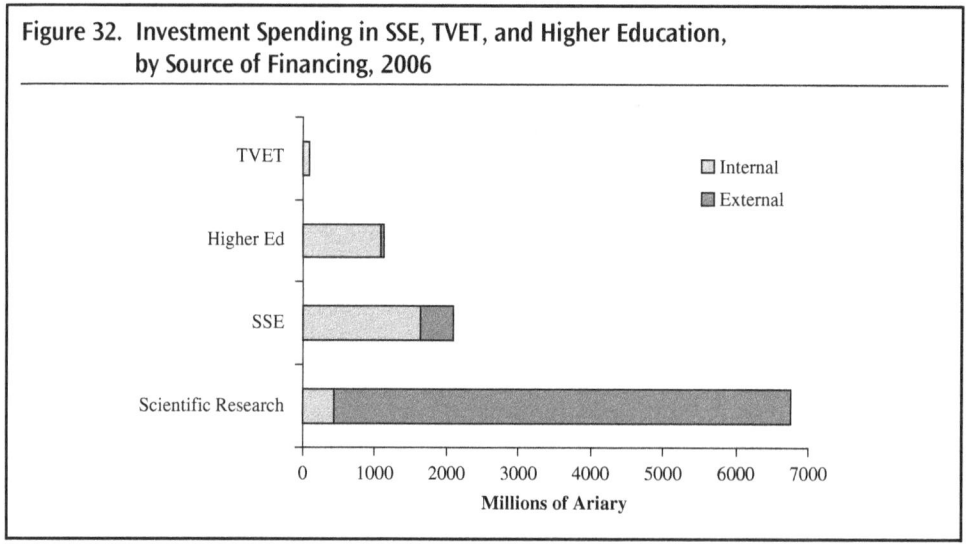

Figure 32. Investment Spending in SSE, TVET, and Higher Education, by Source of Financing, 2006

Notes: Budget execution data.
Source: MEN 2008a: Mise en œuvre du plan Éducation Pour Tous : bilan annuel 2007. March 2008, Annex 1.

Table 12. Per Student Public Recurrent Expenditure, by Level of Education, Constant 2006 Prices

(000s Ariary)	2002	2003	2004	2005	2006	Average Annual Increase
Primary	45.4	44.3	42.7	46.4	43.4	See note 1
JSE	135.7	161.3	133.9	147.2	117.2	−3.6%
SSE	340.5	396.5	320.4	370.9	344.4	0.3%
TVET	519.4	526.9	660.6	598.9	387.6	−7.1%
Higher Education	948.3	804.7	896.7	806.6	1065.7	3.0%

Note: 1. Average annual increase is not calculated for primary education to avoid misinterpretation of data, as a significant part of current expenditures (e.g., community teacher remuneration) is financed by expenditures classified as investment in the budget.
Source: MEN, 2008b. *Rapport d'Etat du Système Educatif National Malgache* (in progress).

salary levels. They are not disproportionate either in relation to per capita GDP or as a ratio of unit expenditure in primary education when compared to many other SSA countries.[26]

Almost all of public recurrent expenditure is on salaries in senior secondary education, leaving about 1 percent on school operating costs. Public schools finance additional inputs through registration fees, which they are free to set. Expenditures on teacher training, curriculum or materials development are notable by their absence (Figure 33).

The disproportionate share of staff salaries in *SSE* highlights the major inefficiencies in public spending at this level—low student-teacher ratios, under-utilization of teachers and a relatively high proportion of administrative staff. The average student: teacher ratio of 20:1 in public secondary schools is lower than the SSA average and arises from the over-specialization of the curriculum and subject overload, small size of schools and low teaching hours. Public SSE teachers' salaries are about 7 times per capita GDP but this is not unusual, given that teachers have university level education. In any case, as their salaries are set as part of civil service salaries, there is little room for maneuver. It does mean, however, that teachers are an expensive resource and must be utilized carefully. Low teacher workload and pupil-teacher ratios are things that Madagascar cannot afford if it wishes to maximize use of its resources. In short, Madagascar's SSE has a high cost structure which is disguised by the low absolute levels of unit costs (in dollar terms).

In *technical/vocational training,* the share of personnel costs is about 78 percent. Student-teacher ratios quadrupled in CFPs from 4:1 to 16:1. This has come about as a result of hiring freeze and has resulted in the aging of the teaching force. Institutions have also increased their size to accommodate enrollment increases. The average size of a public vocational training center grew from 34 students in 1999 to 138 in 2005, when new constructions were restricted. However, average teaching loads at about 20 hours per week are about 50 percent lower than international averages.

---

26. Per student recurrent expenditure in primary education is understated in the table, which uses the budgetary classification, because of some recurrent expenditures are on the investment budget. Adjusting for these would give ratios of per student expenditure at each sub-sector that are in line with norms for low-income countries.

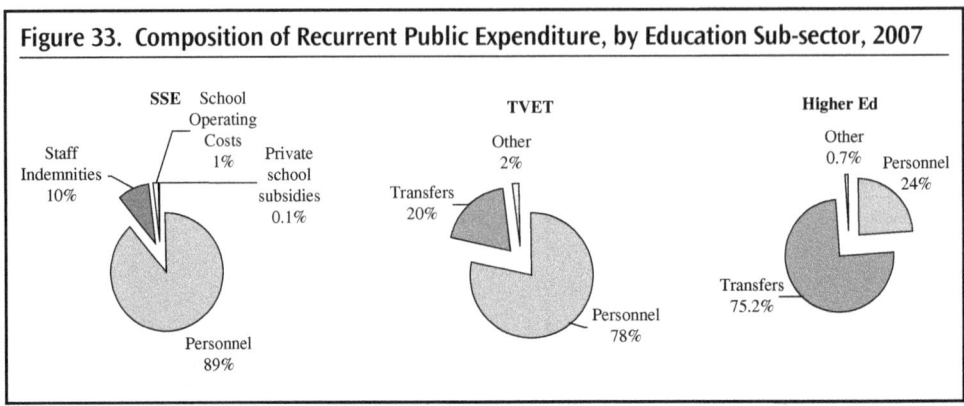

Figure 33. Composition of Recurrent Public Expenditure, by Education Sub-sector, 2007

Notes: 1. Transfers to institutions are for public TVET schools and higher education institutions, which manage these funds. For latter, this includes payment for supplementary hours of university faculty. 2. Data are for budget execution (commitment basis), provisional estimates.
Source: Zaafrane 2008.

About a quarter of the public budget is transferred to public training institutions for supplies. These institutions are therefore relatively better funded than SSE. Further, training institutions are allowed to mobilize additional resources.

In *higher education*, salaries of permanent teaching staff are included in the Ministry of Education's budget and paid directly by the Ministry of Finance. This accounts for a quarter of recurrent expenditure. Three-quarter of the expenditures consists of transfers to public institutions, which are managed by them. The transfers include a variety of expenses, including supplementary teaching hours of faculty, salary of non-teaching staff, operating costs (pedagogical and overheads) as well as domestic scholarships to students. Universities account for over 80 percent of all transfers (Figure 34).

A better economic classification of recurrent expenditure in higher education is obtained by breaking down transfers into their components. This shows that about 54 percent of

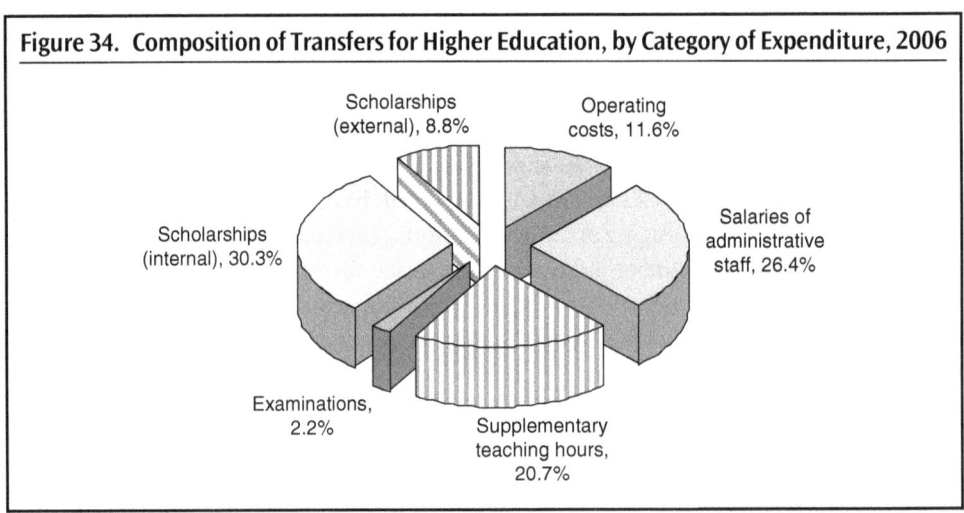

Figure 34. Composition of Transfers for Higher Education, by Category of Expenditure, 2006

Source: Zaafrane, 2008.

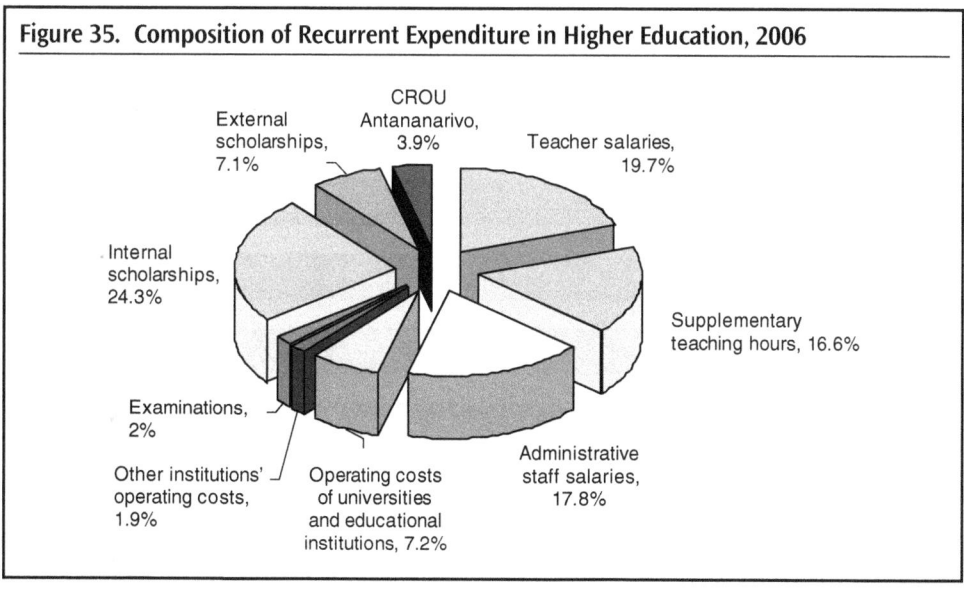

Figure 35. Composition of Recurrent Expenditure in Higher Education, 2006

Source: Zaafrane, 2008. Note: CROU is the *Centres Régionaux des Œuvres Universitaires,* the organization in charge of student dormitories and canteens at the University of Antananarivo.

current spending comprised remuneration of staff, two-thirds of which is spent on teachers (salaries and complementary hours) and the rest on administrative staff (Figure 35). About 30 percent of total recurrent spending was allocated to scholarships, leaving only 10 percent for administrative and pedagogical expenses of universities.

Universities manage about 80 percent of public funds for education and their spending patterns in 2006 underscore serious deficiencies in the use of resources:

- About one third of a university's budget goes to the central administration (Presidencies) of universities, another third to the actual teaching institutions and a third to scholarships.
- Four items comprise most of central administrative expenditures: the salaries of non teaching staff hired by the university (32 percent); petrol and travel costs (15 percent); water and electricity (10 percent) and student accommodation, exams etc (25 percent). Faculty training accounts for just 1 percent of central expenditures.
- About half the expenditures in the faculties/teaching institutions are on scholarships and another 25 percent on supplementary teaching hours and temporary staff. Ten percent is on administrative staff.
- Very little is spent on faculty development or research by either the central administration or teaching institutions. The Presidencies spent less than $5,000 in total on faculty development and about $350,000 on research. In the faculties and institutions, another $100,000 was spent on faculty training and $200,000 on research.
- Per student spending on administrative and pedagogical expenditures was only US$ 65 per year. This is a grim indicator of the reality in Malagasy higher education institutions, which lack basic teaching-learning materials.

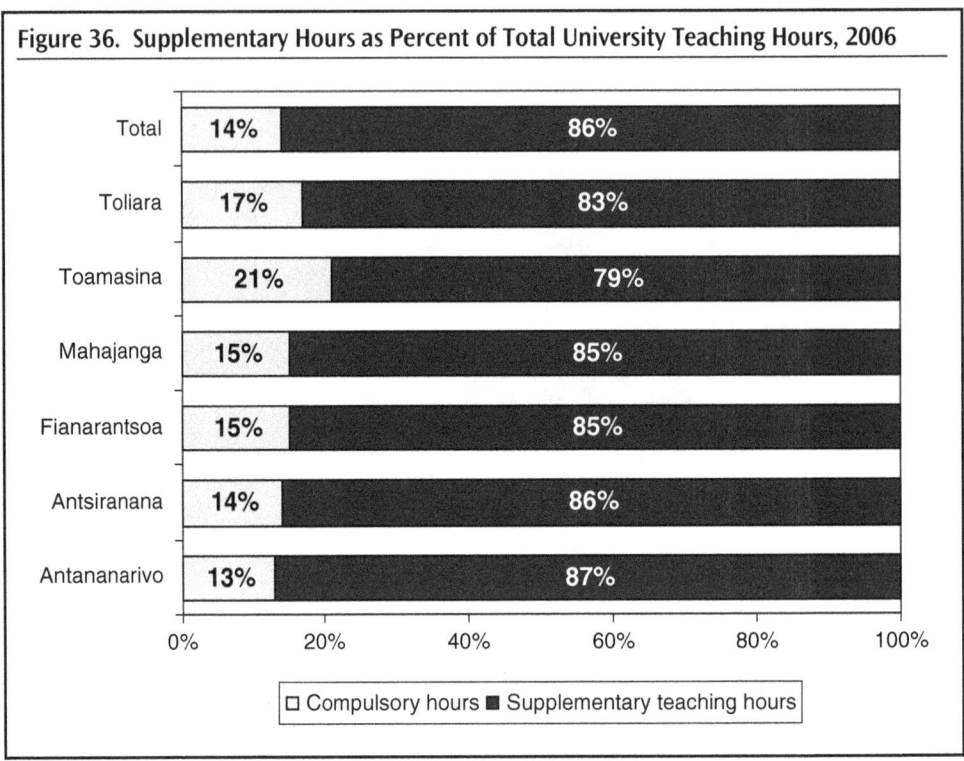

Figure 36. Supplementary Hours as Percent of Total University Teaching Hours, 2006

Source: Zaafrane, 2008.

The case of supplementary teaching hours reflects graphically the inefficiency of public spending. Since 1992, a hiring freeze on university teachers has resulted in an explosion of supplementary teaching hours, which now account for almost 85 percent of total hours taught (see Figure 36). This is a result of several factors. First, professors and assistant professors have a very light teaching load of 5 hours per week. The original justification for this (that faculty would spend about 15 to 20 hours on research) does not hold any more, as the conditions for research do not exist. Second, there is little administrative control in terms of procedures and criteria for determining supplementary hours of teaching. The hourly rate for supplementary teaching hours increased by 174 percent between 2002 and 2007. As a result, faculty earn almost as much from supplementary hours as from their regular salary. The supplementary teaching hours are not distributed across departments and individual faculty members according to transparent criteria. Overall, this phenomenon has a negative impact on the quality of teaching and research as faculty members are keen to increase their remuneration by accumulating supplementary hours. Further, it creates a strong vested interest to protect existing teaching-learning processes for fear that teachers' earnings may be disrupted.

Salary Level of University Teachers

A review of faculty remuneration and recruitment procedures should be a high priority in the medium term to ensure effective functioning of universities. The original aim of the hiring freeze was to control salary expenditures in the early 1990s, so that Government resources could be focused on managing the macroeconomic crisis occurring during that time. Since then, and long after the macroeconomic crisis abated, the Government has maintained the hiring freeze and system of supplemental hours. As a result, there is not enough new faculty to accommodate increased student enrollments—and existing faculty fill this gap by teaching costly "supplementary hours" above their regular salary. The average annual salary of university teachers was about US$6100 in 2007, which is about 17 times the per capita income. In real teams, salary levels have remained roughly constant this decade. This salary does not include additional revenue from the supplementary teaching hours, which may double the remuneration of some teachers (mainly senior faculty members). Hence, university teachers are relatively well paid in Madagascar. Excluding supplemental income, they get 3.4 times more than civil servant primary teachers and 2.5 more than secondary teachers. However, in absolute terms and in relation to norms in SSA countries, the salary levels are low and may be insufficient to attract good faculty. The critical issue, however, is that a significant part of the earnings of university teachers is distributed without proper regulations or control. Even more than in the case of SSE, teachers are the most expensive resource and their workload and performance are critical to increasing the overall effectiveness of higher education.

Another source of inefficiency is the high ratio of administrative staff to faculty. At the University of Antananarivo, for instance, there is an administrative staff of 2,200 for about 500 teaching staff, or one administrative staff for 11 students. Public institutions have a much higher proportion of administrative staff, ranging from one staff for 6 to 16 students, compared to 1:18 in private institutions.

One of the major differences between Madagascar and most other African francophone countries is that, since the mid 1990s, the Malagasy tertiary education institutions have not been directly involved in financing and managing subsidized restaurants and dormitories for the majority of students. On the positive side, this means that the social expenditures part of the tertiary education budget is less sizeable than in other francophone countries. The Ministry of Education department (CROU) operates facilities only in the University of Antananarivo.

However, the negative side is that most institutions do not have adequate provision for basic student services. The living conditions in all university student hostels are inadequate, from the viewpoint of space, hygiene and safety. Transportation services are minimal. In those institutions which have dormitories, students use electric stoves at the university's cost. This practice is so widespread that electricity costs represent 42.5 percent of the total budget of CROU, the Ministry of Education department responsible for social services. The electricity issue often becomes a source of conflicts with the students, as mentioned earlier in relation to the problems of insufficient budget allocation to pay the arrears and delays in disbursements.

Principal Issues in Resource Utilization

Senior Secondary Education

The critical size of SSE schools is around 275 students, below which number, the unit costs of students grows at a geometric rate. Sixty percent of SSE schools have enrollments of less than 200. The small size of schools accentuates the problems of teacher underutilization caused by low teaching load per teacher and too many subjects. Seventy percent of SSE schools have fewer than 20 students per teacher (World Bank 2008). The proposed re-structuring of curriculum provides an opportunity for better deployment of polyvalent teacher and increasing their workload to international norms. It should also enable increasing the size of schools, at least in urban and semi-urban areas. A school construction strategy, built on the lessons learned from the national construction strategy for basic education, would help to optimize school sizes and ensure good construction. To do so, it should include clear planning and technical norms, as well as identification of the number of new classrooms required.

Higher Education

This sub-sector also suffers from the small size of institutions. Only two universities (Antananarivo and Toamasina) have the minimum enrollment size to qualify for a multi-faculty university, which is resource intensive in terms of administration. Despite the lack of critical mass, five out of the six universities offer postgraduate programs. Enrollment in these programs is very small, ranging from 4 to 10 percent of total enrollment. Paradoxically, the share of postgraduate enrollment at the University of Mahajanga is almost twice that at the University of Antananarivo, which is supposed to be the main research institution in the country.

There are many cases of duplication among existing schools and institutes within the universities. The University of Antsiranana, for example, has two technology-focused institutions, the *Ecole Supérieure Polytechnique* and the Technical Teacher Training Institute ("*Ecole Normale Supérieure Technique*"), which have a lot of comparable courses. Similarly, the Faculty of Sciences' business administration department overlaps with the newly created Business Administration Institute. At the University of Antananarivo, the Faculties of Humanities and Sciences and the Teacher Training College offer many similar courses. It seems that schools, institutes and departments are often created on an ad-hoc basis, without a strategic vision of how each university should evolve. An example of resource sharing is provided in Antsiranana where the Technology Institute and the Polytechnic work well together, sharing professors and lab facilities.

Budget Management

As is common in francophone countries, the Ministry of Finance exercises strong ex-ante control over the major categories of the budget both at the time of the preparation and execution. The move to "program budgets" since 2005 is intended to introduce greater flexibility in budget management, by allowing greater discretion by the Ministry to re-allocate within the main programs. In the case of the education sector, these programs correspond to the sub-sectors. However, in practice, there continues to be a clear separation between the preparation and reporting of the three main components of the budget, personnel expenditures, non-personnel current expenditures and the public investment program (PIP). The first is managed directly by the Ministry of Finance, while the last is driven by donor projects. The fungibility of resources within a broad program (for instance, senior secondary education) is accepted by the budgetary law but not implemented in execution, as prior controls still exist at the level of budget line items.

There are major weaknesses in budget preparation in post-basic education. This arises primarily from a lack of policy and clear medium-term priorities for each sub-sector. Another contributing factor is the lack of planning and technical capacity to prepare the budget according to priorities, including lack of tools. The Ministry has benefited from technical assistance financed under Bank's Governance and Institutional Development project, pro-actively used it with Bank support especially in context of EFA. Concrete advances have been made through the preparation of sector policy note and medium term expenditure plan, which is updated annually and used for budgetary discussions with the Ministry of Finance and trade-offs in making sub-sectoral allocations.

However, the advances have been relatively limited in post-basic education in comparison with primary education. In the latter, budget preparation tools have been created, including use of the personnel database, calculation of unit costs, planning of construction. An annual performance plan is prepared for EFA and the Ministry is moving towards similar tools for individual technical directorates and the regional and district offices. In contrast, budget preparation in the post-basic education is still in incremental mode, with little link to strategic objectives.

Budget execution still poses major problems, despite considerable efforts by the Ministry of Finance to simplify procedures. A study commissioned by the Bank in 2005 in the context of public expenditure found that release of expenditures often required up to 18 signatures. Further, the period of budget execution is effectively limited to 6–7 months, with commitments beginning only in April and ending by October/November. The Ministry of Finance imposes limitations on budget execution in the first six months due to lack of domestic revenue in that period. Reform of budget execution procedures, which should complement the move to program budgets, have not been implemented effectively, due to lack of clarity and training of Ministry of Finance staff in the districts, software problems, etc. The focus is still on the control of inputs, rather than on the management and utilization of resources.

The third area of budget management, reporting, is arguably the weakest, especially in post-basic education. The Ministry submits a report to the national assembly on the realization of physical targets but not on budget execution. Within the Ministry, regular reports are not prepared or reviewed for management purposes. The exception is the EFA program, where as part of the joint donor reviews, bi-annual performance reports are prepared, which cover the results indicators, budget execution, progress in implementation of key activities, new initiatives and institutional performance. A positive feature of the EFA reports is the discussion of problems and challenges in program implementation.

There are several problems in budget reporting. As expenditures on personnel are controlled by the Ministry of Finance, the Ministry of Education does not track either the number of staff or expenditures (except in the case of primary education). Expenditure on transfers, which represent a significant part of the higher education budget, are not tracked at all, because they are managed by the institutions. As stated earlier, these transfers finance the supplementary teaching hours of faculty (which are almost equal to faculty salary expenditure) as well as the salaries of administrative staff of universities. Universities submit reports to the Director of Finance in the Ministry of Education, but these are not analyzed.

This lack of reporting and review explains why key expenditure items have grown uncontrollably and why universities can continue for years without paying the electricity bill. The government also does not assess the resources generated of autonomous organizations, such as universities, and the expenditures financed them.

Reform Priorities

Improving Resource Utilization

In senior secondary education, key policy decisions are required to improve resource utilization at the system level. The first is to improve teacher utilization, which could be done through the introduction of reform of curriculum. The second is to plan carefully the distribution of schools. The World Bank's report on secondary education suggests that there are economies of scale up to an enrollment size of 275 in senior secondary schools. This is clearly more applicable in urban areas. In rural areas, with dispersed populations, models for rural schools and alternative delivery mechanisms must be found.

In TVET, the most important way to make more efficient use of existing resources is to shorten the length of training.

In higher education, the non viable size of most universities and the dispersion of resources across a relatively large number of post-graduate programs call for two types of government decision. First, the Ministry of Education should assess, for each of the four under-populated universities, the feasibility of expanding enrollment to at least 5,000 students. Those universities where this goal is not achievable in the near future could be downgraded and should operate as a single or several regular institutes. Second, postgraduate programs should be consolidated in one or two universities at most to start taking advantage of economies of scale.

In order to optimize, the utilization of existing facilities and available resources, each institution should undertake a strategic planning exercise to rationalize the existing offering of programs and courses and guide the development of new programs in years to come. Additional funding could be made conditional on universities undertaking such an exercise, for which technical assistance should be organized.

The issue of supplementary teaching hours requires addressing the employment conditions and status of faculty as well as general civil service remuneration conditions. The most feasible course is to introduce new conditions for new faculty hires in priority courses, including higher salaries tied to a new system of performance evaluation that would take their actual teaching and research output into consideration. The example of Pakistan is worthy of study, where a parallel tenure track was established for new faculty with higher salary and stricter productivity requirements. Participation by higher education institutions is voluntary, but those participating would get additional funding. Any steps to reform faculty recruitment and remuneration should ensure that the best faculty will be retained and rewarded—to enhance the overall quality of university instruction, and to make sure that teacher training is high quality.

While the State should not get involved again in the direct financing of social services for all students, each tertiary education institution could facilitate, through sub-contracting arrangements with private firms or agreements with the relevant municipalities, the organization of basic social services for the students. Successful experiences, such as the non-subsidized cafeteria managed by the Student Association at the Antananarivo Technology Institute, should be studied carefully and emulated.

In all sub-sectors, improvements in internal efficiency through reduction of dropout, repetition and failure on examinations, will release financial and physical resources.

Encouraging Resource Mobilization in Public Institutions with Greater Accountability

Currently, resource mobilization is important only in TVET and in higher education. However, it can be expanded even in SSE, through for instance, setting up a textbook and learning materials fund at the school level, which would pool resources from the government, households and private contributions. Increasing the use of learning materials is critical to improving quality and the Ministry should avoid the temptation to provide all these free of cost. Measures for cost-sharing should be accompanied by targeted aid for poorer students.

In TVET, the possibility of expanding employer financing should be actively pursued, but this would also required setting up governance structures that allow employers to manage funds. A study on financing options should be considered, including a national payroll levy, voluntary contributions, or sectoral funds for skills development.

In higher education, resource mobilization activities and the use of these additional resources are got governed by clear rules. The share of non-budgetary resources has increased to about 10 percent of resources of universities. Registration and other fees account for close to 60 percent of their resources. Revenues from consultancy services and others constitute less than 10 percent. The "payment courses" account for another 31 percent and are growing rapidly.

The first task is for the Ministry of Education to provide all public tertiary education institutions with a clear description of applicable regulations and procedures as defined by the Ministry of Education itself, the Ministry of Administrative Affairs and the Ministry of Finance. Each tertiary education institution, in turn, will need to work out appropriate criteria and mechanisms for the allocation of income among all entities concerned (university/institute/school, department, individual). In many tertiary education institutions in industrial countries, additional income is split equally among the three levels.

Reforms in Public Resource Allocation Mechanisms

Resource utilization and mobilization, as well as changes in the educational process and outcomes, can be induced by the conditions under which public funds are provided to institutions. In senior secondary schools, the introduction of school development funds for quality improvement can be used to leverage changes teaching-learning, improvement in internal efficiency and ensure better budget management and reporting. In order to be successful, the program requires clear guidelines, schools need to be supported with technical assistance for the preparation of development plans as well as in implementation, and there should be effective monitoring.

In both TVET and higher education, the Ministry should consider transferring incremental resources to public institutions on the basis of performance, rather than historical levels. Three main types of innovative allocation mechanisms might be considered in this context (examples given relate to higher education but can be adapted for TVET):

- *Output-based funding formulas:* Funds for recurrent expenditures (part or total) would be given based on a formula linking the amount of resources spent on inputs such as the number of students or professors to some indicator of institutional performance such as the number of graduates. Sometimes higher amounts are paid for graduates in certain fields of study, or with specific, high-priority skills.
- *Performance contracts:* governments enter into regulatory agreements with institutions to set mutual performance-based objectives, relating to fields of study, efficiency indicators or resource utilization.
- *Competitive funds:* financing is awarded to peer-reviewed proposals designed to achieve institutional improvement with respect to quality and relevance, promote pedagogical innovation and foster better management. Institutions are typically invited to formulate project proposals that are reviewed and selected by committees of peers according to transparent procedures and criteria. The eligibility criteria vary from country to country and depend on the specific policy changes sought, for example, whether to change whole universities or individual faculties.

The capacity of the Ministry to design and implement such reforms needs to be built. Funding formula, for instance, require detailed data on factors that affect cost. In order for competitive funds to be effective, apart from clear and simple criteria and procedures, an independent evaluation committee is required. In countries like Madagascar that have a relatively small or isolated academic community, it would be desirable to draw from a regional or international pool of peer reviewers to reduce the danger of complacency and subjective evaluation among a limited group of national colleagues. Use of a transnational pool is a long-standing practice in the Scandinavian countries, the Netherlands and Ireland.

In addition to changing the resource allocation mechanisms, the Government needs to clean up the arrears situation in universities for utilities, such as electricity. This may require action by the Ministry of Finance, rather than the Ministry of Education.

The Ministry should also demand greater accountability for the use of all public resources as part of the move to new allocation mechanisms. Improving the regularity and content of normal budget reporting would greatly help. The Ministry's directorates responsible for SSE, TVET and higher education should show monthly and quarterly reports on financial execution, as well as bi-annual and annual performance reports assessing the progress in implementing the program and problems encountered. The EFA implementation reports already provide a model within the Ministry. In addition, all public institutions, starting with universities, but eventually all senior secondary schools should be required to submit at least one annual report on their activities and use of funds.

CHAPTER 8

Steering Change
Reforms in Management and Governance

The post-basic education system must be re-oriented to respond to labor market and development needs. The re-orientation requires important changes in how education institutions and the overall post-basic system are managed and governed. Institutions need to become more outwardly oriented. To do so, they must be given greater flexibility while being made more accountable for results. This requires changes in organizational structures and mandates. At the same time, the education and training system as a whole needs mechanisms for goal setting and policy making, and structures and instruments to motivate institutions to change and to foster partnership with economic producers. This chapter examines these issues, first identifying key reforms at the system level and then identifying reforms specific to each sub-sector.

Building Mechanisms for Political Leadership of the Reform

Involving the users and other stakeholders of the education and training system—especially employers, but also private institutions, other Ministries, teachers, and so forth—is extremely important. Because of the time required to show results, experience shows that education reforms succeed only if reforms enjoy broad support across the political spectrum.

To achieve broad support for reform, many countries have established higher level bodies, above the Ministry of Education. These bodies report to the Prime Minister or President's office. They might establish policy, commission studies, ensure inter-Ministerial coordination, organize consultations, or guide the use of additional funds towards national priorities. Examples from other countries include commissions for specific sub-sectors (higher education; secondary education; skill development), or broader "knowledge commissions" or "education commissions."

Madagascar could consider establishing a commission for post-basic education along these lines (Box 6). However, it is important to assess the feasibility of doing this, given the administrative capacity at various levels, and to avoid creating large bureaucratic structures. The responsibilities of such a body should be clearly delineated, with a nimble governance structure that is appropriate to these responsibilities.

Irrespective of the option chosen for leading the reform, it is important to establish mechanisms for involving actors outside government, for consultation as well as for assistance in taking key policy decisions. If establishing a national commission is not appropriate at this stage, the Ministry could consider creating task forces on specific issues, the members of which would be drawn primarily from outside the education system. An alternative is to establish a leading body for specific sub-sectors that require a high degree of external participation (for example a National Training Authority for TVET—see below). The most important challenge for the Ministry of Education is to become more outwardly oriented by listening to the needs and demands of the society.

Box 6. Model for a Post-Basic Education Reform Commission

International experience has shown that reform commissions are helpful in driving successful educational reform. A reform commission typically provides oversight, ensures progress against reform benchmarks, and offers guidance on critical areas of reform—or bottlenecks that appear during implementation.

A Post-Basic Education Reform Commission (PERC) might help to establish accountability for successful reforms in secondary and higher education in Madagascar. An important issue to consider is who the Commission should report to. Some countries have found it useful to have the commission report to the President or Prime Minister. Another issue is the responsibilities given to the commission. Some possibilities include:

1. Policy research and development
2. Curriculum development and assessment policy
3. Regulation of private secondary schools and universities
4. Management of Funds for School/University Development/Training funds and Scholarships
5. Management of donor-financed technical assistance
6. Management of monitoring and evaluation of reforms
7. Creation of National Qualifications Framework.

The PERC could be authorized to receive funds from domestic and international sources, both public and private. It could be empowered to contract for both long term and short-term technical services.

The PERC's Board of Governors could be made up of a cross-section of stakeholders affected by post-basic reform. A sample mix could be private industry (relatively high representation) public sector ministries, the private schools sector, local government and education officials Governors could serve terms such that 1/3 of governors will be appointed every three years. The Board would elect its own chairperson every two years.

In this framework, the MEN would continue to be responsible for teacher salary administration, school construction, routine monitoring and evaluation, and all functions related to basic education.

Redefining the Role of the Ministry of Education

The Ministry of Education does not play a leading role in steering the sector. There is as yet no policy or strategy for senior secondary education, TVET or tertiary education. Many of the weaknesses discussed below result from this. There is limited capacity to develop policy, operational strategies and implementation plans. Nonetheless, the example of EFA shows that both leadership and planning/operational capacity can be built through a structured process of "learning by doing" together with international technical assistance.

One major issue preventing more rapid capacity building is the frequent change of the organigram, and accompanying change of senior personnel. In 2002, the creation of a single Ministry for education, through merger of three separate Ministries for school education, TVET and higher education, respectively, created the possibility for a holistic policy for the sector. However, this has not materialized in practice. Although the Ministries were merged, there was no rationalization of functions and human resources. In the last year there have been three major re-organizations, mainly affecting post-basic education. The departure of key personnel with each re-organization results in loss of capacity as there is no institutional memory. The organizational instability reflects in part the lack of strategic direction.

Problems of governance and management are more complex in higher education and TVET, because these sub-sectors involve interface with stakeholders outside the education system and steering institutions that have a high degree of autonomy in many respects. It is particularly due to these reasons that reforms in these sub-sectors have been difficult to conceptualize and implement.

The Ministry lacks a cadre of professional educational administrators, which modern education systems require. Most staff view their job functions as being related to executing the budget or managing personnel files. Most staff are teachers who have taken up administrative positions. University faculty who work in the Ministry also continue their teaching and research duties.

There is no simple panacea to these problems. Major organizational re-structuring is not a solution in and of itself. However, it is advisable to carry out an institutional assessment of main structures and work processes in the Ministry and to identify capacity building measures for key functions such as planning, budgeting, human resource management and project management. Based on this, a capacity building program can be created. The most important mechanism for capacity building, however, is through the practice of designing and implementing reforms. Limited capacity means, however, that priorities should be chosen very carefully.

As a first task, the Ministry could constitute a dedicated team with an appropriate skill mix, including members drawn from outside the Ministry and the education sector, to develop a long term vision and strategy for higher education. Policy options should be formulated based on the analytic work done so far. These options should include choices regarding structure, curriculum and course duration and the priority programs that are demanded by the country's development strategy. The feasibility of these options should be evaluated through (i) financial and fiscal sustainability analysis using medium-term projections of expenditures and resource availability and (ii) consultations with stakeholders. This could be followed up with the design of operational programs and reforms to implement the strategy.

Creation of a Madagascar National Qualifications Framework

An important priority to ensure the outward orientation of educational and training institutions is the establishment of a national qualification framework that ensures that all Malagasy educational and vocational qualifications are clearly understood by students and their families, employers and society at large. A National Qualifications Framework could provide a hierarchy of educational qualifications that clearly describes the knowledge and skills gained from each post-basic education award, and the equivalency between awards. It could serve as a consistent framework that employers could use to identify prospective employees' knowledge and skills. It would also allow educational institutions to design admission criteria, curriculum, teaching methods and student assessment/exams to different skill standards. Such frameworks improve access and mobility by enabling a wide recognition of learning achievements obtained through different sources.

The creation of such a framework will take several years and international experience indicates that it is necessary to start with a simple framework. However, all frameworks involve some common steps:

- Industries identify relevant occupations and the skill and knowledge requirements required to carry out the jobs
- Curriculum, teacher training and learning materials required to meet the skill standards are developed by education and training institutions
- Accreditation is done by government or industry to certify that the education and training programs meet these skills standards
- A hierarchy of qualifications is defined, with inputs from stakeholders, to determine equivalence and progression.

Commitment to the framework by employers is essential to ensuring that education institutions and students use it to for designing and choosing programs. Many countries have found it useful to establish a national qualification agency or authority to develop and implement the framework. This option requires developing a clear mission, roles and responsibilities and appropriate governance structures. However, creating an agency within the Ministry of Education to start the process and organize consultation with employers is a viable option, to build up support and avoid creating bureaucratic structures that do not have a clear mission.

Governance and Management Reforms by Sub-Sector

Despite some changes introduced since the 1990s to encourage institutional autonomy, Madagascar's education system suffers from major deficiencies in governance and management. There are, however, good examples within Madagascar which should serve as guideposts for the future. International experience with implementing education reforms is also useful.

Senior Secondary Education

The positive feature of the public *lycées* is the existence of a school council, comprised of the school head, representatives from parents and teachers and local authorities. The school council has authority to set fees but in practice it does not influence the functioning of the school. The school has little recurrent budget. Teachers are recruited and deployed by the central Ministry. Principals are appointed by the Ministry, without specific training. Supervision responsibilities are assigned to the *Direction Régionale de l'Education Nationale* (DREN); they often have no means to carry out supervision and little capacity.

At the Ministry level, capacity gaps are glaring. There is no unit responsible for curriculum development, teacher training or student assessment.[27] The directorates have had no experience in developing policy or in planning.

The introduction of school development funds and/or scholarship programs, discussed earlier, provides an opportunity to address all these issues on a manageable scale. The design of these programs should assign specific roles and responsibilities to different levels, right up to the school principal and school council. Leadership training and capacity building should be built into the program. The creation of new types of schools should be linked to developing planning capacity for determining the location and type of schools.

Vocational and Technical Training

There are several positive features in the organization and management of institutions, as a result of reforms of the 1990s. First, TVET institutions have autonomy to select entrants, to set fees and spend the revenue in line with approved work programs and government regulations. There exist structures that enable employers to interface with government. This includes, at the regional level, the organization of training providers, employers and government (*Groupement d'Etablissements Educational, Technique et Professionnelle*—GEETP) and the National Council of Technical and Vocational Training (*Conseil National de la Formation—Technique Professionnelle*—CNFTP) at the national level.

However, there are also many weaknesses. Structured participation by employers to direct the TVET system and to express their need for workers of different skills is limited. Even in the GEETP, employers represent only 30 percent of the group. Another weakness is that various Ministers are involved in TVET provision and regulations with limited coordination. Apart from MEN, there are the Ministry of Labor, which sometimes provides approvals for new institutions, and other sectoral Ministries that operate sectoral training institutions.

The government should create a mechanism for establishing close linkages with the labor market and employers. The latter have to be involved at various stages of the process, from identifying priority areas to exercising quality control. One possibility is to establish a National Training Authority (NTA). The NTA would include providers, government and employers and enable the latter to articulate their training requirements. It would establish policies and standards, monitor performance, provide accreditation and quality assurance and allocate funds for training. Another model followed in some countries is to establish

---

27. A unit for development of curriculum, learning materials and assessment has been created in the Directorate-General for Education for All and has responsibilities for basic education.

"sector councils" especially in priority economic sectors. Such councils bring together the three main stakeholders and sometimes workers' representatives to assess human resource needs and shortages of specific skills and find solutions. A third model is to link the assessment of training needs directly with investment promotion, particularly in order to attract FDI. The agency that solicits FDI would also assess skills gaps and propose measures for skills training either through domestic providers or in partnership with the foreign investor.

An important issue is whether the Ministry of Education alone can take leadership in constituting a body involving cross-sectoral coordination. Experience in other countries suggests that the involvement of higher levels of the political leadership is required to jump-start the process.

Higher Education

The institutional governance and management mechanisms in universities are not in line with international trends. However, Madagascar does have tertiary level institutions that are managed well, use their resources effectively and produce good results.

University Boards, established in the 1990s, have not been functioning well. They have little representation of industry and limited mandate. Their main function is to approve the budget and oversee its execution. During the 1990s, university presidents were nominated by the government from three candidates proposed by the University Board. Currently, the universities adopt a democratic approach, in which the faculty and administrative staff elect their leaders. However, the selection does not guarantee that only the most competent candidates are selected due to the lack of comprehensive criteria.

Management practices in the public universities are ineffective from the following reasons: (i) their management information systems including accounting and financial reporting and performance related data management are weak; (ii) university heads lack leadership; (iii) most universities do not make enough efforts to develop proactive strategies and long-term vision—only a few schools have accepted to introduce a self-assessment process; (iv) there are little linkages with industry; and (v) universities lack a culture of management flexibility and responsiveness to demands.

By contrast, the two ISTs have better, functioning Boards, which have equal representation from the public and private sectors, and are actively involved in strategic planning on management and providing effective support to strengthen linkages with firms. The directors of the two ISTs are appointed by the Minister of Education based on merit criteria.

An important area of inflexibility is the management of faculty positions and remuneration. The former is controlled by the Ministry of Finance and the latter is defined by civil service laws and regulations. All public tertiary education institutions—universities and technology institutes alike—are heavily constrained in making decisions on the number of teaching positions they need, and do not have the possibility to offer competitive compensation packages both to keep their brightest faculty members and to attract the best internationally. Nor are they able to offer other incentive packages to attract faculty of their choice locally or internationally.

Four areas of reform appear to be the priorities. First, the Ministry of Education should move from direction management functions to strategic functions such as vision setting, medium term planning, guidance on development priorities and related training needs, resource allocation to stimulate quality improvements, career guidance and information management. Table 13 summarizes the desirable changes.

Table 13. Two Scenarios for Government Regulation

Areas of oversight and regulation	Present situation	Proposed approach
Formulating overall vision and setting policies	Y	Strengthened
Allocating budgetary resources based on performance and equity criteria	N	Y
Evaluating and promoting quality	Limited	Strengthened
Allowing flexibility to hire and dismiss faculty	N	Y
Allowing flexibility to establish salary levels	N	Y
Imposing ex ante financial controls and audits	Y	N
Allowing flexibility in procurement rules	N	Y
Monitoring / evaluating	Limited capacity	Y

Source: Salmi, 2008.

Second, to facilitate the financing reforms proposed in the previous sections, the Ministry of Education could grant increased management autonomy to the public tertiary education institutions under its authority. These would be accompanied by agreed performance objectives and greater accountability. The use of a competitive fund could be one vehicle for introducing these management changes.

A third area of reform is to modify the composition and powers of university boards as well as the mode of appointment of the university leaders. A single tier board is increasingly become common growing number of countries (the Anglo-Saxon model, as compared to the two-tier structure that was common on the European continent), which combines both supervisory and executive (managerial) tasks. Such boards have extensive powers, including overseeing all financial management aspects, selecting the president/rector, determining the appointment and employment conditions of staff, and deciding on the management of the property of the university.

A fourth area is to move ahead with the new accreditation system for both public and private institutions. However, the proposed new regulations would benefit from external peer review in order to ensure that the conditions are appropriate for Madagascar, including the need to have a diversified system that can expand access. One way of dealing with the heterogeneity of the Malagasy tertiary education system would be to establish different criteria for different types of institutions.

CHAPTER 9

A Strategic Framework for Post-basic Education in Madagascar

This work is the first stage in development of a strategic framework for post-basic education reform, based on sound policy choices and strong consensus around those policy choices. The next steps are to agree upon the over-arching components of reform; design the specifics of the reform initiative; and phase them at a measured pace during the implementation phase. This chapter reviews the analytical inputs provided in this report, and outlines the reforms implied by the report's analysis.

Overview of Report Findings

Rationale for Reform

There are two main rationale for reform of Madagascar's post-basic education system. First, Madagascar may not be able to reach its MAP goal of 8–10% annual GDP growth by 2012 without a significant increase in the quality and educational attainment of its labor force. Last reformed in the 1970s, post-basic education is not relevant to current or future labor market demands. Madagascar's educational attainment is markedly lower than that of other lower income countries. Indicatively, 11% of Madagascar's labor force has secondary education or higher—against 15% in Pakistan, 17% in Bangladesh, 22% in India, and a striking 53% in Sri Lanka. Madagascar's average educational attainment declined slightly between 2001 and 2005, from 4.1 to 3.9 years. For Madagascar to have a strong foundation for growth, this trend must be reversed.

Second, post-basic education reforms are required to provide a broader segment of Madagascar's youth the opportunity to build core labor market skills and, consequently, participate in the benefits of Madagascar's growth. Today, post-basic enrollment is strongly biased towards students in upper income quintiles and select geographic regions. In 2005, average JSE enrollment for the bottom 3 income quintiles was 13 percent, against 38 percent for the top income quintile. Average SSE enrollment for the bottom 3 quintiles was 1 percent, against 14 percent for the top income quintile. Inequality in post-basic education enrollment perpetuates economic disparities and has the potential to erode social cohesion.

State of the Current System

The post-basic education system needs a major overhaul. The education provided is poor quality. As mentioned above, post-basic education is not relevant to current or future labor market demands. The post-basic education system also has poor "throughput," or ability to move students successfully from matriculation to eventual graduation. There are high rates of drop-out, repetition and exam failure. As a result, 45 students must enroll in Grade 6 (JSE) for a single student to complete tertiary education. As highlighted above, enrollment is especially low—and "throughput" weak—for students in lower income quintiles and disadvantaged geographic regions.

Drivers of Weakness of the Current System

There are two main reasons for the weakness of the current system: (i) poor governance and (ii) financial inefficiency.

In terms of governance, Madagascar has first and foremost lacked the decisive political leadership that is needed to drive major reform. There is no coherent post-basic education strategy. As a result, it is very difficult to build a cohesive post-basic education system. MEN's organizational structure is frequently changed, which has made it hard to assign and maintain clear accountability for performance of the post-basic education system. Lastly, there is no "feedback loop" between MEN and the private sector, which prevents MEN from developing a post-basic system that is relevant to current or future economic needs.

In terms of financial inefficiency, the current system is both under-funded and high cost. Though Madagascar's total education expenditure is on par with that of other low income countries, 59 percent of spending was allocated to basic education in 2006. The share of public expenditure allocated to post-basic education (at 5.5 percent for SSE, 2.3 percent for TVET and 15.6 percent for tertiary) is below average for SSA or francophone countries. Furthermore, these resources do not stretch very far because (i) the teacher payment structure drives high staff expenditure (indicatively, 98.7 percent of SSE and 78 percent of TVET recurrent expenditure are spent on personnel costs and other staff payments), and (ii) the structure and specialization of the curriculum increases teacher and classroom requirements.

Reform Priorities

Key Reform Areas

The goal of Madagascar's post-basic education reform is to build a high quality post-basic education system, that is, a set of institutions that provide students with multiple pathways to post-basic education, that provide differentiated skills to the labor market, and that support Madagascar's economic development needs. A secondary goal is to increase access to post-basic education, especially for students from the bottom 3 income quintiles and from disadvantaged geographic regions.

There are three areas in which reform is required: (i) educational content (structure, curriculum, teaching, and process) and linkages with the economy; (ii) cost-effective increases in coverage; and (iii) the enabling framework for reform (finance, governance, and sub-sector management).

Educational Content. The objective of content reform is to ensure that educational content equips students to respond to current and future labor market demands. There are three major elements of reform. First, the post-basic education curriculum must be simplified and made more relevant to current and future labor market needs. Changes might include a reduction in subject overload, the re-organization of the technical and academic *baccalauréats* into more relevant tracks, and on-going private sector input into curriculum development and modification. Second, reforms must aim to improve teacher quality at all post-basic levels—in SSE, in TVET and in tertiary education. In SSE, reforms could include in-service teacher development, aimed at improving classroom instruction and familiarizing teachers with new curriculum; design of a teacher certification that could be open to all bachelor's or master's degree holders, not only those studying pedagogy at the university level; and expansion of university capacity to train a larger number of teacher educators. At the tertiary level, reforms should change faculty recruitment, focusing on recruitment in priority areas such as math, science, and languages; faculty hiring, with permanent contracts granted only after the completion of a successful trial period; and faculty development, with workshops designed to upgrade faculty skills in the short term, and research support provided in the long term. Third, incentives to enhance tertiary institutions' performance are needed. These might include the creation of competitive research funds, or increases in funding tied to clear performance benchmarks.

Increased Coverage. Increased post-basic coverage aims to raise the educational attainment of the labor force, and to reduce inequalities in enrollment and completion across income groups and regions. To a large extent, coverage will rise naturally as the quality of post-basic education improves. Additional measures will that could drive further increases and greater equity in coverage include: (i) more effective cost management, with a focus on rationalization of school sizes and shortening of TVET training; (ii) enhancement of scholarship programs' equity and efficiency, including definition of stricter, needs-based eligibility criteria, increases in scholarship levels to cover students' actual living costs, exploration of the feasibility of a student loan program, and introduction of needs-based scholarships at the secondary level; (iii) launch of open and distance learning (ODL) programs, focusing on selection of an appropriate ODL model for Madagascar; and (iv) greater private sector provision of education, beginning with clarification of the rules for private sector participation in post-basic education, and creation of state and local subsidies to enhance participation.

Strengthened Enabling Framework. A stronger enabling framework is *critical* to post-basic education reform—Madagascar's past reform experience suggests that reform will not succeed without a strong and clear enabling framework. This framework has three elements.

First, clear, emphatic political leadership of reform is central to reform success. The government must be strongly committed to reform, and that commitment must be reflected in a public policy document and other concrete actions. High-level and broad-based political support must be systematically built. The creation of a mechanism for political leadership of the reform and steering the post-basic system is required. A post-basic education reform commission with high level political authority and involving outside stakeholders should be considered. The role of the Ministry of Education needs to be re-defined, depending on the option chosen.

Second, there must be a strong governance framework for reform. The governance framework must include a post-basic reform strategy for the medium term which guides budget allocations and other actions; a National Qualifications Framework, so that post-basic qualifications correspond to labor market needs and are recognized by employers; and decentralization of some decisions to the district or school level, accompanied by funding to support those decisions.

Third and finally, stronger financial management is required. Better financial management includes upgrading financial management capabilities; rationalizing capital investment decisions (schools, classrooms, teachers) based on defined utilization and equity criteria; and increasing funding to post-basic education through greater private sector participation and user fees.[28] Reform should clarify the rules around resource mobilization, so that it is clear how resources can be raised, used and reported on.

General Principles of Reform

Successful post-basic education reform will keep the post-basic "system" in balance. To design such a reform, that will keep the system in balance, policymakers must ensure that:

- Reforms in SSE, TVET and higher education are consistent with one other, and with basic education reforms.
- Reforms strike a balance of power between the national post-basic education system, and the institutions that will carry out the reforms at the regional and local levels. The national system should provide the context and incentives for the regional or local institutions, while local institutions will need the autonomy, access and resources to carry out reform.
- Reforms are phased in gradually with individual institutions, to allow implementation capacity and consensus to be built, and adjustments are made to implementation as experience is gained.
- The education sector—and MEN in particular—becomes more outwardly oriented, actively seeking the participation and cooperation of individuals and organizations outside the sector in designing the program.
- The pace of expansion in coverage calibrates the availability of financial resources against physical and managerial capacity, to ensure the feasibility and sustainability of reform.
- Technical expertise is used to design key elements of reform, such as those related to governance, financing and curriculum changes. These reforms should not be launched in an *ad hoc* manner without preparation.

---

28. A national school construction strategy—building on the experience of national school construction strategy for basic education—could help to rationalize capital investment decisions related to schools and classrooms.

Cost of Reform

An important step in development of the strategy is to cost the proposed reform measures. The final selection of policies will be greatly influenced by the availability of resources. Of special importance are policies related to the structure and duration of courses, teacher numbers and salaries, and the cost of facilities and equipment.

Specifically, the Ministry needs to assess the cost implications of different post-basic reform scenarios. It must weigh the advantages of each reform scenario against its cost, taking projected domestic resource availability and external funding into account. Cost estimates must take both investment needs and recurrent expenditure needs into account.

Alternative scenarios could be developed using a simulation model constructed around four basic modules: (i) enrollments (including coverage and completion, student flows between and within each education level); (ii) service delivery parameters, such as curriculum structure and specialization, student-teacher ratios, types of schools, etc; (iii) costs, specifically costs of construction, equipment, teachers' salaries, scholarships or student aid, and system-level management; and (iv) financing, specifically public resources, private resources and external donor funding. Differences in targets for each scenario are incorporated through varying assumptions in each module.

The Ministry has experience in preparing and using simple models for projecting financial requirements in basic education. However, at the post-basic level, more detail is required in order to take into account the higher level of complexity of the system, and the diversity of courses and institutions. Cost estimates can be sensitive to assumptions regarding student flows through these different channels. Further, the directorate of planning in higher education is not adequately staffed, and currently there is no unit dealing with planning of senior secondary and TVET.

In the short run, technical assistance should be used to build a simulation model for post-basic education. The simulation model will allow policy makers to assess the impact of key options. The results of these simulations should be used to guide selection of the final policy options. Over the medium-term, the capacity for system planning and financial projections should be built within the Ministry.

Next Steps and Time Frame

Madagascar should develop an overall strategy for post-basic education, using the elements described in Table 14 as priorities. The suggested framework, presented in Table 14, focuses on five pillars. The first two pillars relate to system level reforms: (i) system governance and (ii) resource mobilization and efficiency. The other three pillars relate to specific reforms in each of the three sub-sectors: SSE, TVET and higher education.

In terms of phasing, the main priorities are as follows:

- *Short term (1–2 years):* (i) determine strategic policy choices; (ii) cost the alternative reform scenarios, to assess the financial sustainability of each scenario; (iii) choose a reform scenario, to guide budget allocation and additional donor funding; (iv) design new governance structures and financing instruments, to orient the system towards labor market needs and to improve equity; (v) launch investment on a modest scale for quality improvement in selected institutions and programs, devolving greater autonomy to institutions; and (vi) diversify types of programs/institutions

- *Medium term (3–5 years):* (i) establish the National Qualifications Framework; (ii) revise the regulatory framework for the private sector, accreditation and other system level structures; (iii) increase the use of performance-based financing instruments to reinforce reforms at the institution level; and (iv) expand the investment program to upgrade quality, create some model new institutions, and enhance access
- *Long term (beyond 5 years):* (i) update the National Qualifications Framework, based on feedback from employers, educational institutions and end beneficiaries; (ii) create governance systems for permanent interaction between MEN and employers, and sustainable financing mechanisms; (iii) ensure all education and training institutions are accredited and become autonomous; and (iv) roll out quality improvement reforms throughout the system and expand access rapidly.

Table 14. Framework for Strategic Development of Post-Basic Education

Short Term (1–2 yrs.)	Medium Term (3–5 yrs.)	Long Term (5+ yrs.)
Objective 1: Effective System Governance		

♦ Formulate draft post-basic education strategy; consult with stakeholders and finalize strategy; conduct specialized studies, including teacher study
♦ Determine the appropriate steering mechanism for the reform, including re-defining role of MEN and new governance structures
♦ Undertake financial simulations to determine feasible policy
♦ Conduct assessment of institutional capacity in Ministry and universities/training institutions
♦ Develop and implement communication strategy
♦ Develop and implement SSE and TVET teacher recruitment and professional development policies
♦ Revise faculty recruitment procedures and professional development for new hires at universities in selected fields
	♦ Give authority to the steering mechanism to channel new funds according to priorities
	♦ Devolve authority to selected institutions in conjunction with new financing instruments
	♦ Develop and introduce management development programs for MEN staff and educational institutions
	♦ Implement key frameworks, based on results of feasibility studies
	  ○ National Qualifications Framework
	  ○ Private sector regulatory framework
		♦ Devolve authority to all universities, training institutions and senior secondary schools
		♦ Update National Qualifications Framework, based on feedback from employers, educational institutions and end beneficiaries

(continued)

Table 14. Framework for Strategic Development of Post-Basic Education *(Continued)*

Short Term (1–2 yrs.)	Medium Term (3–5 yrs.)	Long Term (5+ yrs.)
◆ Undertake key feasibility studies 　○ National Qualifications Framework 　○ Private sector regulatory framework, including changes required for accreditation, quality assurance, and partnership with foreign providers		

Objective 2: Enhance Resource Mobilization and Efficiency

Short Term (1–2 yrs.)	Medium Term (3–5 yrs.)	Long Term (5+ yrs.)
◆ Assess possible scope of private sector participation, including private sector market size, growth and business model ◆ Develop planning criteria to rationalize location of public schools and university programs, giving weight to regional equity criteria ◆ Prepare simple tools for budget preparation and reporting at MEN level ◆ Create system of monitoring efficiency	◆ Design and launch competitive funds/performance-based funding/scholarship funds to improve quality, target equity and leverage managerial change in secondary schools, TVET and universities ◆ Strengthen budget management capacity in MEN ◆ Strengthen financial management and reporting capacity at the institution level	◆ Design and introduce new system of transfers of public funds for improving performance and internal efficiency ◆ Create fund for long-term development of post-basic education or for specific sub-sectors with multiple sources

Objective 3: Expand Higher Quality Senior Secondary Education

Short Term (1–2 yrs.)	Medium Term (3–5 yrs.)	Long Term (5+ yrs.)
◆ Undertake study to re-organize/modernize *baccalauréat* series ◆ Review curriculum in priority areas and identify needs for learning materials and equipment ◆ Undertake study of teacher preparation and development needs ◆ Design and launch scholarship program for poor students	◆ Expand school provision, school development fund and scholarship program ◆ Continue revision of curriculum ◆ Establish model senior secondary schools ◆ Determine new types of secondary schools for expansion in rural areas, and for specific regional/skill needs as well appropriate open learning systems ◆ Design and start implementation of school development fund for selected public and private schools	◆ Introduce open learning system in selected areas ◆ Roll out the reform to all SSE schools ◆ Introduce changes to examination and assessment system

(continued)

Table 14. Framework for Strategic Development of Post-Basic Education *(Continued)*

Short Term (1–2 yrs.)	Medium Term (3–5 yrs.)	Long Term (5+ yrs.)
Objective 4: Improve Relevance of Skills Training		

♦ Take a policy decision to introduce vocational course after grade 10 and phase out existing CFP
♦ Undertake tracer study on TVET graduates
♦ Evaluate the current provision and training needs for the informal sector
♦ Review curriculum for LTPs in priority fields
♦ Expand training to enterprises
	♦ Create mechanisms for identifying national/regional/sectoral training needs and rationalize role of MEN and Ministry of Labor
	♦ Pilot promising institutional models and curriculum
	  ○ Revised vocational and LTP curricula in selected institutions
	  ○ Model TVET centers
	  ○ Experimental models for informal sector training
	♦ Redesign vocational training and SSE technical training to be shorter and more flexible (polyvalent; multi-purpose institutions)
	♦ Introduce revised pre- and in-service instructor training
	♦ Increase financing for instructor training and move to demand-side financing
	♦ Institutionalize graduate tracer studies
		♦ Implement re-designed vocational training courses in priority fields
		♦ Design and implement employer participation in testing and certification of graduates
		♦ Establish national skills development authority based on lessons learnt
		♦ Upgrade curriculum in all vocational centers and LTPs
		♦ Expand informal sector training based on the outcomes of experiments and trials

Objective 5: Create a High Quality Tertiary Education System		
♦ Conduct assessment of labor market needs with employers and other government agencies and enrollment/cost projections to determine the relative priorities and quantitative targets for specific disciplines, types of programs and institutions ♦ Undertake feasibility study of expansion of ISTs in different regions and begin investment ♦ Undertake feasibility study of expanding/specializing regional universities and provide additional funding ♦ Prepare plan for introducing LMD reform and start introduction ♦ Undertake study of private sector, external partnerships and open/distance learning	♦ Reform university governance structures ♦ Expand number of ISTs, based on need and available funding ♦ Roll out LMD implementation in more disciplines using competitive funds or other financing mechanisms ♦ Expand Ph.D training and faculty development programs ♦ Establish accreditation and quality assurance mechanism for public and private sector ♦ Introduce new open/distance learning delivery systems to expand access ♦ Design and start implementation of competitive fund in selected institutions/disciplines ♦ Design and start implementation of revised student scholarship scheme	♦ Increase tertiary enrollments through diversified system of public universities, ISTs, private sector, foreign partnerships and ODL ♦ Continue upgrading of curriculum in different fields ♦ Introduce benchmarking of institutions against international standards ♦ Design mechanisms for university-industry partnerships, and provide matching funding to encourage applied research partnerships in selected priority fields

APPENDIX

The Reform of Basic Education in Madagascar

Lessons and Implications for Post-basic Education

Madagascar's education and training system has to respond to three challenges: (i) make education and training more relevant to labor market needs; (ii) increase access in a cost-effective manner; and (iii) improve equity through more balanced regional development and creating opportunities for poor students.

Reforms to address these concerns in an inter-related manner are already advanced for the new basic education cycle (grades 1–10). These include:

- Changing the structure and duration of education cycles—this enables an increase in access and internal efficiency, while improving relevance.
- Introducing reform of curriculum and pedagogical practices—this is closely linked to the reform of the structure and duration and is imperative for increasing relevance and quality.
- Providing alternative and flexible delivery models that complement the formal education system.
- Targeted programs to improve enrollment and completion.

This chapter briefly assesses the important changes in basic education and the lessons and implications for the reform of post-basic education.

Proposed New Structure of School Education

The school cycle in Madagascar currently comprises five years of primary, four years of junior secondary, and three years of senior secondary education. This system, with a relatively long junior secondary duration which is typical of francophone systems, is due to change between

2008 and 2011. The primary cycle will be gradually extended to seven years of education, with a lower primary sub-cycle of five years and an upper primary sub-cycle of two years. The junior secondary phase will become three years of duration and together, the primary and junior secondary cycle will constitute a basic education cycle of 10 years. These reforms are in line with international trends, where countries are increasingly moving to universal provision of 9 or 10 years of education with a common curriculum.

The new senior secondary education will last for two years and entrants to senior secondary education will therefore have ten years of prior schooling. Technical and vocational education and training (TVET) will also undergo a change. Currently, students can enter vocational training after grade 5, if they fail to enter junior secondary education. The reform means that students would enter vocational programs after 7 or 10 years of schooling, depending on the choices made regarding the introduction of vocational reforms.

The reform of primary and junior secondary education is well articulated in the Ministry's new EFA Plan, *Plan d'Education pour Tous*. The plan includes EFA 10, the 10 year basic education cycle (Figure 37). Funding of the reform will be provided by the government budget and through a US$85 million grant from the Education for All–Fast Track Initiative global partnership, which has been secured for the period 2009–11. Introduction of the new primary cycle is expected to begin in September 2008, with the new grade six being introduced in 20 districts and new curriculum and textbooks introduced in grade 6 and grade 1 in these districts. The reform will be rolled out to new districts and new grades in a phased manner. The reform of junior secondary education will begin on a small, experimental basis in 2009 and will be scaled up, depending on implementation capacity and availability of resources.

In the vision for EFA10, the outcomes of ten years of good quality education for all are directly linked to strengthening the human resources needed for the nation's economic growth strategy. The Ministry has used the reform to introduce major changes in curriculum, language of instruction and teacher training and textbooks.

The new curriculum will be structured around three main domains of learning: (i) Malagasy and social studies (ii) mathematics, science and technology and (iii) other languages (French and English). These domains will organize teacher and student time, learning materials and the participation of the local community is thus of critical importance to improving quality. This new curriculum will replace the highly academic and increasingly irrelevant one installed at the time of independence.

Figure 37. New Structure of Basic Education

CYCLE	Primary (Basic Ed – 1st Cycle)			Junior Secondary (Basic Ed – 2nd Cycle)	
COURSE	1st	2nd	3rd	4th	5th
GRADE	1 2 3	4 5	6 7	8 9	10

Reform of Primary Education

At the primary level, a new curriculum with use of Malagasy as language of instruction in grades 1–5 and strengthening of language teaching in French and English (upper primary) is being designed (Figure 38). The curriculum renewal is complemented by new learning materials, new teacher education and certification programs as well as school-based teacher development initiatives. Changes in management and governance with progressive expansion of regional, district and school budgets are being introduced.

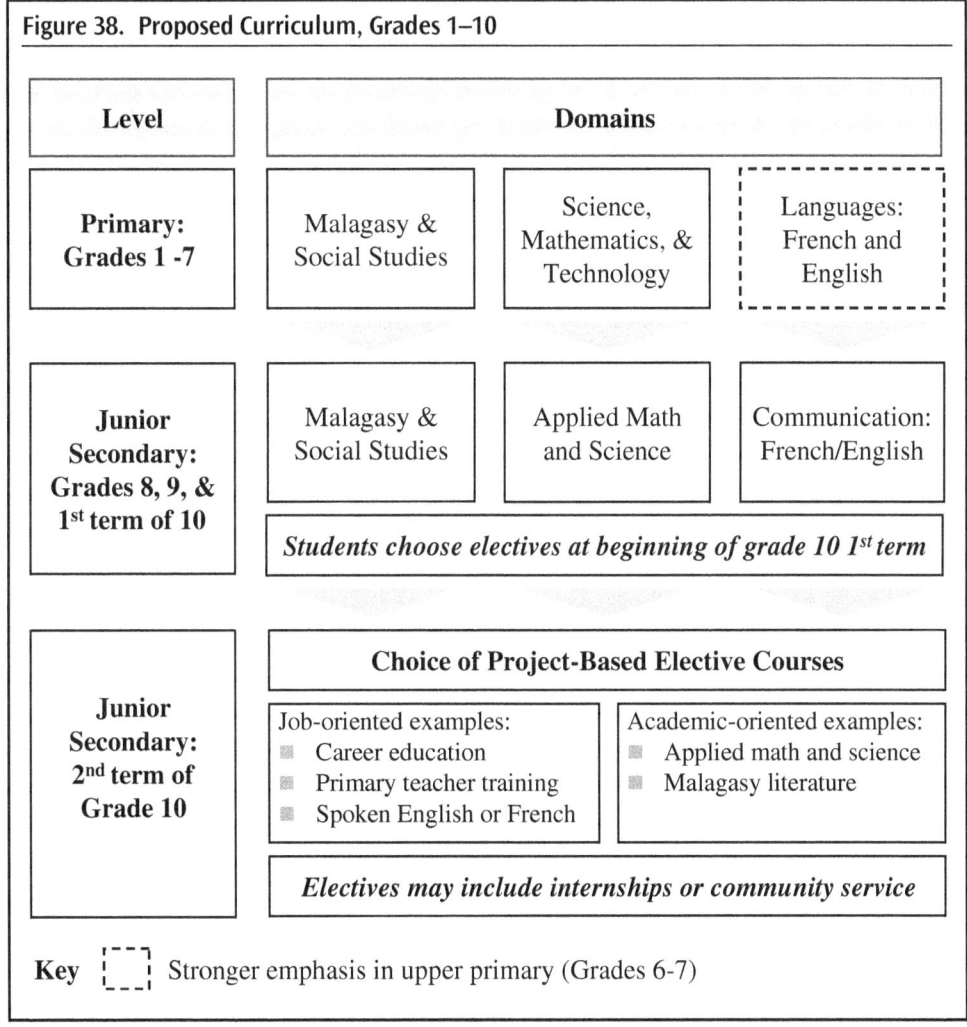

Figure 38. Proposed Curriculum, Grades 1–10

Source: Adapted from Middleton (2007), Figure 1.

Reform of Junior Secondary Education

The challenges for junior secondary education are to equip students for the triple requirements of the world of work, society and senior secondary education. The reform of junior secondary education will focus on three broad areas: (i) quality improvement through curriculum reform, new teacher training programs and learning materials and (ii) creating high quality junior secondary schools (*collèges d'excellence*–COE) networked with other JSE schools and (iii) expanding access through introduction of flexible learning models.

Curriculum

The new JSE curriculum would depart from the traditional model currently in use. The general trend in the world is to move to a reduction of subjects and curriculum overload. Currently, Madagascar's JSE curriculum requires about 1100 class time a year, significantly higher than the 800–1000 hours norm in most OECD countries and other regions that are modernizing their curriculum. This long duration, together with a framework that emphasizes rote learning, reduces time for self-directed student learning.

The new curriculum would be aligned with the curriculum domains of the new primary curriculum, and it would use Grade 10 to broaden and deepen student learning to include 21st century skills in problem solving, critical thinking and communication (see Figure 38, above).

Collèges d'excellence (COE) and Network Schools

COEs would be the focal point for introducing new curriculum, distributing learning and training teachers. COEs would provide leadership and support a network of four to six local schools while the new curriculum and teaching methods are put in place. COE teaching loads would include in-service work with teachers of other schools, in their classrooms as well as in their own classrooms. Changes would be disseminated through the network schools. Implementation would be based on voluntary participation of public and private schools, which would receive additional funding and technical support.

This is a "whole school" development approach. It is a departure from the traditional model of grade-by-grade curriculum change which is appropriate for the primary level. This approach allows scaling up according to implementation progress and building up capacity gradually.

Teacher Training

The curriculum reform implemented through the COEs would be supported through renewal of teacher training programs at the senior secondary and university levels. The programs will focus on teacher verbal ability, knowledge of the content being taught, and mastery of teaching methods. In Madagascar's context, the following teacher competencies are especially important: multi-grade teaching, how to adapt the general curriculum to rural realities and needs; the ability to teach across the courses in a curriculum domain and to work as a team with the head teacher and other teachers, with parents and with community leaders; the skills to organize open schools, to design elective courses; and to organize and supervise student community service and work internships.

Flexible Learning Modalities

Open schools would be introduced to provide flexible learning opportunities for those who have completed primary education but are unable to continue with formal education or those who have discontinued JSE. Many countries, including India, Indonesia, and Colombia, and nearly all OECD countries as well, have established Open Schools that enable students who cannot attend regular schooling to study for their examinations. Successful approaches emphasize flexible student promotion, a curriculum oriented to rural issues, special learning materials, specially trained teachers and high levels of community participation. Open schooling has much to offer in Madagascar. Lessons of experience also show that large scale and rapid expansion of a "packaged" model without careful management and monitoring is risky. Flexible, community-based models work better. These elements are expected to be built into the open school model at the JSE level.

Improving Equity

The EFA 10 program envisages targeted measures to improve access and completion, with the goal of ensuring universal primary completion by 2015 and gradually expanding junior secondary. At the primary level, these include ensuring that all villages are provided with a complete lower primary cycle (grades 1–5) within a radius of 2 km, allowing flexibility in the school calendar based on local climatic conditions, providing targeted funding for districts with low completion rates and funding to schools to improve school level management. At the JSE level, greater equity in geographical coverage will be a criteria for new schools (especially public schools) and funding for private schools will encourage participation of poor children. Open schools are another method to expand educational opportunity.

Implications and Lessons for Post-Basic Education

Overall, the reform of the basic education structure and simplification of the curriculum resulted in cost savings in two main areas: construction and specialized teachers. These resources can be used for expanding access and improving quality.

The reform of basic education has implications for other levels. The first is an opportunity. Extending universal primary education to 7 years and basic education to 10 years, which increasing number of children will complete over the next decade, will itself raise the educational attainment of the population. Introducing flexible opportunities for out-of-school youth will enable faster progress on this. Curricular reform can improve the competencies of the majority of young people who will enter occupations in agriculture and the informal sector. The implication is that, while access to post-basic education will need to increase to absorb a part of the increasing number of JSE leavers as well as for Madagascar's growth strategy, the main focus of the reform in the medium-term can be on improving quality and relevance for skilled labor needs and supporting economic development.

The second implication is that reform of post-basic education cannot be avoided, if only to avoid discontinuities in the system. As a starting point, programs at the tertiary level would need to be changed in order to upgrade the quality of teachers at the lower levels. More importantly, a holistic approach to the content of education is required across the spectrum. Finally, reform at the higher levels is required to broaden the base of support for reforms at lower levels of the education system.

There are also some important lessons. Beyond the primary level, the implementation of reforms is best done through the institutions, rather than launching system wide changes at one go. This is best exemplified by the reform of JSE. Complicated reforms with too many elements are difficult to manage, especially in a low capacity environment. At the same time, reforms focusing on improving quality and relevance need to cover an entire package—curriculum, teachers, learning materials, financing and management—if they are to bring about desired changes in the classroom. Major cost reductions can be realized through curriculum re-organization, utilizing teachers and classrooms more effectively. Careful planning and realistic phasing are important.

Finally, ownership and leadership by the Ministry is required to guide the process of change, which covers both technical and political aspects. For the EFA 10, a considerable amount of international technical assistance is being provided by the partners, but without the leadership of the Ministry's EFA team and a systematic approach to capacity building, these advances would not have been possible. Capacity can be and has been built in the process of leading change.

STATISTICAL ANNEX

Annex Table 1. Public and Private Enrollment by Educational Sub-Sector, 1997–2006

Grade level	1997–98	1998–99	1999–00	2000–01	2001–02	2002–03	2003–04	2004–05	2005–06	2006–07
Pre-school*	108.947			42.383	45.387	93.168	142.750	132.504	146.284	148.356
Public	1.090						14.690	8.644	8.405	8.706
Private	50.946						128.060	123.860	137.879	139.648
Private (other)	56.911									
Primary	1.892.943	2.018.707	2.208.321	2.307.314	2.409.082	2.856.480	3.366.462	3.597.731	3.698.906	3.835.716
Public	1.468.211	1.571.282	1.708.835	1.808.428	1.892.801	2.274.443	2.715.526	2.916.089	2.983.383	3.102.833
Private	424.732	447.425	499.486	498.886	516.281	582.037	650.936	681.642	715.523	732.883
Junior Secondary	258.934	273.613	287.873	316.390	343.937	356.973	420.592	486.239	581.615	660.448
Public	145.652	151.296	159.504	175.069	193.091	201.357	241.213	281.322	341.441	402.077
Private	113.282	122.317	128.369	141.321	150.846	155.616	179.379	204.917	240.174	258.371
Senior Secondary	61.233	60.597	66.381	66.021	77.655	79.238	88.857	106.595	116.794	127.789
Public	31.217	31.571	35.243	33.716	41.702	42.386	46.664	54.000	56.275	58.712
Private	30.016	29.026	31.138	32.305	35.953	36.852	42.193	52.595	60.519	69.077
TVET**	8.741	10.617	12.088	13.558	14.590	15.880	15.820	17.497	20.957	19.178
Public Junior Secondary	1.380	2.217	2.046	1.875	2.264	3.261	3.610	4.174	5.105	5.223
Public Senior Secondary	7.361	8.400	10.042	11.683	12.326	12.619	12.210	13.323	15.852	13.955
Estimated private sector										34,250
Higher Education	16.270	17.887	18.227	31.893	31.905	35.476	42.143	44.948	49.734	57.717
Public institutions	16.270	17.887	18.227	21.599	22.607	26.343	31.675	34.746	39.078	45.491
Non-university institutions				442	485	565	746	794	879	980
Distance education				6.891	6.245	5.935	6.457	5.978	5902	6.885
Private institutions				2.961	2.568	2.661	3.265	3.430	3875	4.361

Notes: *Partial count. **Data excludes apprentices, 2006–07
Source: MEN, 2008b

Annex Table 2. Schools and Teachers by Cycle

	2001/2002	2002/2003	2003/2004	2004/2005	2005/2006
Number of public schools	15,324	15.546	16,346	16,879	18,027
Primary	14,436	14,637	15,420	15,890	16,917
Junior Secondary	780	801	817	875	992
Senior Secondary	108	108	112	114	118
Number of private schools	4,849	5,363	5,858	6,227	6,227
Primary	3,859	4,340	4,740	4,946	5,301
Junior Secondary	739	795	862	980	1,133
Senior Secondary	251	228	256	301	332
Number of public teachers	46,875	49,583	58,550	60,930	70,445
Primary	36,181	38,509	47,320	48,870	57,028
Junior Secondary	8,055	8,390	8,910	9,400	10,603
Senior Secondary	2,639	2,684	2,620	2,660	2,814
% Community teachers					
Primary	n/a	18	28	33	50
Junior Secondary	n/a	n/a	11	12	20
Senior Secondary	n/a	3	5	7	n/a
Number of permanent teachers in private schools	22,656	25,197	29,300	32,300	33,991
Primary	14,555	16,800	16,950	18,270	19,807
Junior Secondary	6,015	6,271	8,950	10,100	10,534
Senior Secondary	2,086	2,126	3,400	3,930	3,650

Source: World Bank 2008. MEN data.

Annex Table 3. Average Years of Education of the Employed Labor Force by Age Group

	2001		2005	
	Average	Standard Deviation	Average	Standard Deviation
15–19	2.6	2.7	3.2	2.6
20–24	3.8	3.5	3.6	3.1
25–29	4.4	3.7	4.0	3.5
30–34	4.8	4.2	4.3	3.5
35–39	5.2	4.5	4.6	3.7
40–44	4.6	4.5	4.3	3.9
45–49	4.3	4.4	4.0	3.9
50–54	3.6	4.1	3.4	3.5
55–59	3.9	4.3	3.3	3.3
60–64	2.4	3.1	2.6	2.8
Total	4.1	4.0	3.9	3.5

Notes: Calculated from *Enquêtes Prioritaires auprès des Ménages* 2001 and 2005.
Source: Lassibille, 2007.

Annex Table 4. Earnings Regression: Salary/Wage Earners,[a] All Sectors, 2001 and 2005

	2001				2005			
	I	II	III	IV	V	VI	VII	VIII
Male	0.187**	0.146	0.1587*	0.172*	0.122*	0.136**	0.1349***	0.146**
Experience[b]	0.027**	0.023**	0.025***	0.026**	0.037**	0.037**	0.036***	0.038**
Experience[2]	−0.000	−0.000	−0.001*	−0.000	−0.000**	−0.000**	−0.000***	−0.000**
Years of Study	0.087**	—	—	0.108**	0.064**	—	—	0.099**
Education Level[b]								
Primary	—	0.222	—	—	—	0.110	—	—
Primary Incomplete			0.068	—			0.052	—
Primary Completed			0.499***	—			0.279**	—
Secondary	—	0.617**	—	—	—	0.374**	—	—
JSE			0.582**	—			0.310***	—
SSE			0.864***	—			0.538***	—
Higher	—	1.054**	1.217***	—	—	0.988**	1.043***	—
Company Size[d] (No. Employees)								
6–10	0.136*	0.157*	0.124**	0.111	0.178**	0.195**	0.182***	0.146*
11–50	0.271**	0.319**	0.272***	0.248**	0.215**	0.234**	0.209***	0.169**
50 and over	0.251**	0.277**	0.253***	0.233**	0.340**	0.380**	0.354***	0.287**
Industry Sector[e]								
Public Admin.	0.248*	0.307**	0.2561**	0.135	0.640**	0.756**	0.692***	0.510**
Industry	0.223*	0.194	0.206**	0.195*	0.326**	0.386**	0.366***	0.287**
Energy	0.387**	0.363**	0.386***	0.353**	0.471**	0.491**	0.448***	0.361**
Construction and Communication	0.408**	0.447**	0.379***	0.323**	0.459**	0.491**	0.472***	0.418**
Transport	0.555**	0.513**	0.522***	0.491**	0.525**	0.591**	0.563***	0.468**
Commerce/Services	0.115	0.112	0.105	0.059	0.117	0.162	0.143*	0.084
Working Hours	−0.000	−0.001	−0.001	0.001	0.006**	0.005**	0.005***	0.006**
Permanent Employee[f]	−0.021	−0.050	−0.022	0.004	0.002	−0.024	−.008	0.013
Rural Area[g]	−0.047	−0.063	−0.050	−0.050	−0.235**	−0.237**	−0.233***	−0.236**

(continued)

Annex Table 4. Earnings Regression: Salary/Wage Earners,[a] All Sectors, 2001 and 2005 (Continued)

	2001				2005			
	I	II	III	IV	V	VI	VII	VIII
Province[h]								
Fianarantsoa	−0.326**	−0.320**	−0.305***	−0.315**	−0.197**	−0.175*	−0.180**	−0.227**
Toamasina	−0.139	−0.100	−0.092	−0.115	−0.038	−0.012	−0.022	−0.083
Mahajanga	0.105	0.159	0.141	0.125	−0.068	−0.040	−0.056	−0.119
Toliara	0.046	0.066	0.047	0.039	−0.225	−0.215	−.0219	−0.263
Antsiranana	0.365**	0.417**	0.394***	0.378**	0.266**	0.288**	0.272***	0.195*
Education–Job Qualification								
Employee Under-Educated	—	—	—	0.202*	—	—	—	0.319**
Employee Over-Educated	—	—	—	−0.321**	—	—	—	−0.208**
Lambda[i]	−0.046	−0.230	−0.142	−0.064	−0.136	−141	−0.129	−0.053
Constant	9.894	10.438	10.184	9.801	9.583	9.720	9.694	9.255
R^2	0.43	0.40	0.426	0.44	0.45	0.44	0.445	0.46
Number of Observations	2838	2838	2838	2838	3784	3784	3784	3784

Notes to Annex Table 4

Calculated from *Enquêtes Prioritaires auprès des Ménages* 2001 and 2005.

* = significant at 10%; ** = significant at 5%.; *** = significant at 1%.

[a] Salary/wage earners, 15 to 64 years. The specifications are such semi-logarithmic; adjustments are weighted. The models adjust for selection bias using the results of the model of choice of employment sector (see Table A6 of Lassibille, 2007).

[b] Difference between the age of the individual (−6) and the number of years of study.

[c] Compared to an employee with no education.

[d] Compared to an employee of a company with 5 or fewer employees.

[e] Compared to an employee of the agricultural and the transport sectors including the communications.

[f] Compared to a contractual employee.

[g] Compared to an employee of a rural area.

[h] Compared to an employee of the province of Antananarivo.

[i] Selection term.

Source: Lassibille, 2007.

Annex Table 5. Earnings Regression: Salary/Wage Earners,[a] Industrial Sector, 2005					
	I	II	III	IV	V
Male	0.068**	0.068**	0.093***	0.113***	0.102***
Experience[b]	0.013***	0.012**	0.013***	0.016***	0.018***
Experience^2	−0.000	−0.000	−0.000	−0.000	−0.000
Years of study	0.056***	0.055***	0.074***	—	—
Education Level[c]					
Primary	—	—	—	0.154**	—
Secondary	—	—	—	0.320***	—
Higher	—	—	—	1.093***	—
Education Level (Detailed)					
Primary	—	—	—	—	0.143**
Secondary (General + Tech/Voc)	—	—	—	—	0.237***
Secondary – Technical	—	—	—	—	0.465***
Secondary – Vocational	—	—	—	—	0.685***
Higher	—	—	—	—	1.090***
Company Size[d] (No. of Employees)					
20–99 Employees	0.046	0.045	0.040	0.029	0.020
99 Employees and over	0.205***	0.198***	0.190***	0.239***	0.216***
Industry Sector[e]					
Food and Drink	−0.353**	−0.368**	−0.288*	−0.073	−0.109
Tobacco	−0.535***	−0.528***	−0.493***	−0.313*	−0.320*
Textiles	−0.353**	−0.371**	−0.261*	−0.033	−0.054
Clothing	−0.341**	−0.357**	−0.269*	−0.087	−0.115
Leather	−0.276	−0.284	−0.217	−0.086	−0.132
Wood	−0.304*	−0.311*	−0.220	−0.040	−0.089
Paper and Plastic	−0.170	−0.176	−0.118	0.018	−0.060
Printing	−0.301*	−0.311*	−0.227	−0.040	−0.118
Chemistry	−0.012	−0.022	0.055	0.186	0.125
Metallurgy	−0.317*	−0.335**	−0.273*	−0.105	−0.188
Machine and Equipment	−0.109	−0.113	−0.005	0.213	0.117
Furniture	−0.135	−0.156	−0.068	0.122	0.049
Construction	−0.165	−0.162	−0.154	−0.041	−0.057
Permanent Employee[f]	0.186***	0.190***	0.184***	0.137**	0.130**
Enterprise Type[g]					
Private Company	0.411***	0.417***	0.328***	0.132	0.147
Single Proprietorship	0.249**	0.250**	0.162	−0.042	−0.034
Partnership	0.287*	0.298*	0.206	−0.096	−0.071
Other	0.275***	0.282***	0.186*	−0.002	0.007

(*continued*)

Annex Table 5. Earnings Regression: Salary/Wage Earners,[a] Industrial Sector, 2005 (*Continued*)

	I	II	III	IV	V
Has Undergone Training[h]	—	0.077**	—	—	—
Employee Over-Educated	—	—	–0.426***	—	—
Constant	11.859	11.865	11.726	12.122	12.186
R^2	0.30	0.30	0.34	0.39	0.42
Number of Observations	1628	1628	1628	1672	1672

Notes to Annex Table 5

Estimated from Investment Climate Assessment Survey 2005.

* = significant at 10%; ** = significant at 5%.; *** = significant at 1%.

[a] People employed. The specifications are such semi-logarithmic; adjustments are made heteroskedasticity.

[b] Real experience since entering the workforce.

[c] Compared to an employee with no education. The secondary education category includes general, technical and vocational education.

[d] Compared to an employee of a company with fewer than 20 employees.

[e] Compared to an employee of the mining sector.

[f] Compared to a contract employee.

[g] Compared to an employee of a public sector company.

[h] Compared to an employee who has not attended any training before the survey.

Source: Lassibille, 2007.

Annex Table 6. Estimated Stochastic Production Frontier Models,[a] 2004

	I		II		III		IV		V	
	Average	Coeff.	Average	Coeff.	Average	Coeff.	Average	Coeff.	Average	Coeff.
Dependent Variable = log value added										
Labor (log)	3.64	0.884***	3.64	0.869***	3.63	0.900***	3.54	1.125***	3.54	1.079***
Capital (log)	5.74	0.212***	5.74	0.200***	5.76	0.135***	5.56	0.075*	5.56	0.081*
Sector (agro-industry = 0)										
Textiles, apparel	—	—	0.27	−0.131	0.27	0.048	0.29	−0.266	0.29	−0.394
Wood and furniture	—	—	0.25	−0.329*	0.24	−0.471**	0.24	−0.467*	0.24	−0.469*
Paper and printing	—	—	0.02	0.213	0.02	0.319	0.01	−1.128*	0.01	−1.025*
Chemicals and pharmaceuticals	—	—	0.07	0.653**	0.07	0.646**	0.07	0.257	0.07	0.144
Metallurgy and machinery	—	—	0.05	−0.262	0.06	−0.485**	0.06	−0.423	0.06	−0.404
Non-metal and plastic	—	—	0.03	−0.353	0.04	−0.409	0.03	−0.840*	0.03	−0.799*
Others	—	—	0.13	−0.192	0.14	−0.194	0.13	−0.392	0.13	−0.426^
Innovative company	—	—	—	—	0.32	0.674***	0.32	0.593***	0.32	0.592***
Female workforce (%)	—	—	—	—	31.97	−0.008**	31.3	−0.007*	31.3	−0.006^
Education level of employees (years)	—	—	—	—	—	—	8.443	0.088*	8.44	0.082*
Provides internal training	—	—	—	—	—	—	—	—	0.31	0.331**
Constant	—	2.137	—	2.384	—	2.678	—	1.563	—	1.694
Lnσ²ᵥ	—	−0.161*	—	−0.243**	—	−0.374***	—	−0.441	—	−0.501
Lnσ²ᵤ	—	−1.045***	—	−0.963***	—	−0.928***	—	−0.930	—	−0.890
Wald chi²	—	274.72***	—	307.44***	—	362.91***	—	332.36***	—	349.23***
Number of observations	152	—	152	—	150	—	117	—	117	—

Notes: *** = significant at 1%.; ** = significant at 5%; * = significant at 10%; ^ = significant at 20%.
[a] Stochastic production function with semi-normal distribution and heteroscedastic variance (variance depending on the volume of sales)

Source: Lassibille, 2008, using an ICA survey data.

Annex Table 7. Public Expenditures on Education by Sub-Sector (Ariary)

(In Ariary millions)	2002	2003	2004	2005	2006	2007
Recurrent Expenditure						
Pre-school	—	—	—	—	—	624
Primary	65336	70985	88918	122271	129472	147623
JSE	18242	28275	24632	37389	40009	46643
SSE	9838	11415	11403	18089	19379	19122
TVET	4331	4510	7970	9137	8123	10187
Higher	21324	19576	26285	35000	52607	52833
Administration	17168	21737	37773	43078	29035	63895
Total	136239	156499	196981	264964	285391	340927
Capital Expenditure						
Pre-school	—	—	—	—	—	1868
Primary	3975	7277	47922	100298	98040	106010
JSE	399	836	2250	3586	379	1796
SSE	907	614	0	4125	2099	4832
TVET	727	668	763	1168	98	493
Higher	8300	14383	5608	14243	7892	6270
Administration	12654	25713	12689	0	753	1427
Total	26961	49509	69232	123420	109261	122696
Total Expenditure						
Pre-school	—	—	—	—	—	2492
Primary	69311	78262	136840	222569	227512	253633
JSE	18641	29111	26882	40975	40388	48439
SSE	10745	12029	11403	22214	21478	23954
TVET	5058	5178	8733	10305	8222	10680
Higher	29624	33959	31893	49243	60498	59103
Administration	29822	47467	50462	43078	29788	65322
Total	163200	206007	266213	388384	387886	463623

Notes: 1. Executed budgets (commitment basis.) 2. 2007 data are provisional. 3. Higher education includes scientific research.

Sources: 1. For 2002–2005, MEN, 2008b. *Rapport d'Etat du Système Educatif National Malgache*. 2. For 2006 and 2007, MEN. 2008a. *Mise en œuvre du plan Éducation Pour Tous- Bilan annuel 2007*. Annex 1. 3. Exchange rates from World Bank Global Development Finance online database.

Annex Table 8. Public Expenditures on Education by Sub-Sector (US$)						
(In US$ millions)	2002	2003	2004	2005	2006	2007
Recurrent Expenditure						
Pre-school	—	—	—	—	—	0.3
Primary	47.8	57.3	47.6	61.0	60.4	78.8
JSE	13.4	22.8	13.2	18.7	18.7	24.9
SSE	7.2	9.2	6.1	9.0	9.0	10.2
TVET	3.2	3.6	4.3	4.6	3.8	5.4
Higher	15.6	15.8	14.1	17.5	27.7	28.2
Administration	12.6	17.6	20.2	21.5	13.6	34.1
Total	99.7	126.4	105.4	132.3	133.2	181.9
Capital Expenditure						
Pre-school	—	—	—	—	—	1.0
Primary	2.9	5.9	25.6	50.1	45.8	56.6
JSE	0.3	0.7	1.2	1.8	0.2	1.0
SSE	0.7	0.5	0.0	2.1	1.0	2.6
TVET	0.5	0.5	0.4	0.6	0.0	0.3
Higher	6.1	11.6	3.0	7.1	3.7	3.3
Administration	9.3	20.8	6.8	0.0	0.4	0.8
Total	19.7	40.0	37.0	61.6	51.0	65.5
Total Expenditure						
Pre-school	—	—	—	—	—	1.3
Primary	50.7	63.2	73.2	111.1	106.2	135.3
JSE	13.6	23.5	14.4	20.5	18.9	25.8
SSE	7.9	9.7	6.1	11.1	10.0	12.8
TVET	3.7	4.2	4.7	5.1	3.8	5.7
Higher	21.7	27.4	17.1	24.6	28.2	31.5
Administration	21.8	38.3	27.0	21.5	13.9	34.9
Total	119.5	166.4	142.4	193.9	181.1	247.4

Notes: 1. Executed budgets (commitment basis.) 2. 2007 data are provisional. 3. Higher education includes scientific research.
Sources: 1. For 2002–2005, MEN, 2008b. *Rapport d'Etat du Système Educatif National Malgache.* 2. For 2006 and 2007, MEN. 2008a. *Mise en œuvre du plan Éducation Pour Tous- Bilan annuel 2007.* Annex 1. 3. Exchange rates from World Bank Global Development Finance online database.

References

Background Papers for this Report

World Bank

d'Aiglepierre, Rohen. 2008. "Enseignement post-primaire privé à Madagascar: Diagnostic de la Situation Actuelle et Analyse des Options Envisageables de Partenariats Public-Privé." Study jointly financed by World Bank and AFD. Unpublished.

Johanson, Richard. 2006. "A Preliminary Assessment of Technical-Vocational Education and Training (TVET) in Madagascar." Unpublished.

Lassibille, Gerard. 2007. "Education et marché du travail à Madagascar." Unpublished.

———. 2008. "La productivité des entreprises malgaches: Résultats d'après l'enquête ICA." Unpublished.

Mikhail, Sam. 2007. "Applied Science, Engineering and Technology (ASET) Education in Madagascar: Analysis of Issues, Challenges and Proposed Reforms Initiatives." Unpublished.

Prasad, S. N. 2007. "Curriculum, Textbooks and Teacher Training in the Indian School System: Study of Four South Indian States." Mysore, India. Unpublished.

Salmi, Jamil. 2008. "Madagascar: Financing and Governance of Tertiary Education." Unpublished.

Ministry of National Education (MEN)

MEN. 2008a. "Mise en œuvre du plan Éducation Pour Tous- Bilan annuel 2007." Draft.

MEN. 2008b. "Rapport d'Etat du Système Educatif National Malgache" (Country Status Report on Education). In progress.

Middleton, John. 2007. "Options for Re-structuring Secondary Education in Madagascar. Discussion Paper for MEN." Unpublished.

Zaafrane, Hafedh. 2008. "Étude sur les coûts et le financement de l'enseignement supérieur à Madagascar." Consultancy Report for MEN. Unpublished.

Other Sources

Alesi, Bettina, Burger, Sandra. Kehm, Barbara M. and Teichler, Ulrich. 2005. *Bachelor and Master Courses in Selected Countries Compared with Germany.* Federal Ministry of Education and Research, Berlin.

Bashir, Sajitha. 2007. "Trends in International Trade in Higher Education: Implications and Options for Developing Countries." World Bank Education Working Paper No. 6, Washington, D.C.

Nathan Associates, Inc. 2006. "Cambodia Garment Industry Workforce Assessment: Identifying Skill Needs and Sources of Supply." Prepared for USAID/Cambodia. Nathan Associates Inc. Arlington, Virginia. Unpublished.

Riboud, Michelle, Yevgeniya Savchenko, and Hong Tan. 2006. "The Knowledge Economy and Education and Training in South Asia: A Mapping Exercise of Available Survey Data." World Bank. Draft.

Salinger, Lynn. 2003. "Competitiveness Audit of Madagascar's Cotton, Textiles, and Garments Sector." Prepared for USAID/Madagascar. Nathan Associates, Inc., Arlington, Virginia. Unpublished.

Shah, Jalan S. A., and Bandar B. Baru. 2005. "Feasibility study for establishing an industry-led skills development program for the textile and garment industry in Madagascar." Penang, Malaysia. Unpublished.

Stifel, David, Faly H. Rakotomanana, and Elena Celada. 2007. *Assessing Labor Market Conditions in Madagascar, 2001–2005.* World Bank, Washington, D.C.

UNESCO. 2002. *Open and Distance Learning: Trends, Policy and Strategy Considerations.* Paris.

World Bank. 2001. "Education and Training in Madagascar: Towards a Policy Agenda for Economic Growth and Poverty Reduction—A Summary of the Key Challenges." World Bank Africa Region Human Development Working Paper Series, Washington, D.C.

———. 2005a. *Expanding Opportunities and Building Competencies for Young People: A New Agenda for Secondary Education.* Washington, D.C.

———. 2005b. *Madagascar: Investment Climate Assessment.* Washington, D.C.

———. 2008. *The Challenge of Expanding Secondary Education and Training in Madagascar.* Washington, D.C.

———. 2008a. *At the Crossroads: Choices for Secondary Education and Training in Sub-Saharan Africa.* The SEIA Synthesis Report, Africa Human Development Series. Washington, D.C.

———. 2008b. *Curricula, Examinations, and Assessment in Secondary Education in Sub-Saharan Africa.* Washington, D.C.

———. 2008c. "Madagascar: Integrated Growth Poles Project." Project Paper. Washington, D.C.

Websites

Bologna Process National Reports website (http://www.bologna-bergen2005.no/)
Global Competitiveness Report 2007–2008 (http://www.gcr.weforum.org/)
National Institute of Open Schooling website (http://www.nos.org/)
UNESCO Institute for Statistics website (http://stats.uis.unesco.org)
World Bank EdStats website (http://sima.worldbank.org/edstats/)
World Bank Enterprise Surveys website (http://www.enterprisesurveys.org/)
World Bank Knowledge Assessment Methodology (KAM) website
 (http://www.worldbank.org/kam)

www.ingramcontent.com/pod-product-compliance
Lightning Source LLC
Chambersburg PA
CBHW081235170426
43198CB00017B/2763